FRENCH FURNITURE

ARMOIRE LOUIS XIV

FRENCH FURNITURE

JACQUELINE VIAUX

Translated by HAZEL PAGET

G. P. PUTNAM'S SONS · NEW YORK

| CONTENTS

4341

LIST OF ILLUSTRATIONS

(All measurements given are approximate)

ARMOIRE, Louis XIV, by André-Charles Boulle. 8 feet 4 inches high; 5 feet 8 inches wide; 1 foot 2 inches deep. Body of ebony standing on plinth decorated with flattened gadroon moulding. Cornice with dentils and lambrequins. Above and below doors are four oblong panels in brass and pewter marquetry on ground of blue-tinted shell. Centre panels in dyed and shaded wood marquetry on dark tortoise-shell ground: vases, bouquets of flowers, birds, butterflies. Bronze mounts chased and gilt: keyhole plates, hinges and rosettes. *Musée du Louvre.* (Photo: Giraudon.) *frontispiece*

PLATE I
CUPBOARD, end of twelfth century. Oak. 7 feet 2 inches high; 7 feet 10 inches wide; 2 feet 8 inches deep. Obazine (Corrèze). Church sacristy. (Photo: Larousse.) *facing p.* 16

PLATE II
CHEST, fifteenth century. Decoration consists of blind Flamboyant fenestration. *Hospice de Beaune.* (Côte d'Or). (Photo: Stévignou.) *facing p.* 17

PLATE III
BUFFET, pinewood, carved, polychrome decoration: 6 feet 10½ inches high; 5 feet wide; 2 feet deep. Single-bodied with two doors; two uprights carved in bold relief with terms supporting capitals; trails of flowers and fruit twine round the tapering columns. A third female-busted term conceals division between two doors. In upper section of doors, two smaller panels decorated at the top with shells and garlands enclose full relief figures of Hercules brandishing his club and Venus standing. In lower section, two polychrome and gilt panels depict the creation of man and the murder of Abel. Attributed to Hugues Sambin, *c.* 1580. *Musée du Louvre.* (Photo: *Connaissance des Arts.*) *facing p.* 24

PLATE IV
BUFFET, double-bodied, Renaissance. Style of Androuet du Cerceau, *Château d'Azay-le-Ferron* (Indre). (Photo: *Musée des Beaux-Arts,* Tours.) *facing p.* 32

PLATE V
TABLE, fan-shaped supports, modern top. From Toulouse workshop. Sixteenth century. Toulouse, *Musée Saint-Raymond.* (Photo: Yan.) *facing p.* 33

7

PLATE VI

CUPBOARD, Louis XIII. South-west France; walnut. Full height: 8 feet 6 inches; Base (1 foot 10 inches high; 6 feet 6 inches wide; 1 foot 10 inches deep) resting on flattened bun feet and containing two drawers; two doors composed of four panels carved in diamond-point design. Heavily moulded cornice (8 inches high; 6 feet 6 inches wide; 2 feet 10 inches deep), decorated with dentil frieze. From Lauzerte (T.-et-G.). Moissac Museum. (Photo: L. Violle.) *facing p.* 36

PLATE VII

CUPBOARD, Louis XIV. South-west France. Walnut. 9 feet high; 6 feet 6 inches wide; 2 feet 2 inches deep. Projecting cornice (5½ inches high), heavily moulded. Two doors comprising four moulded panels; drawer at base extends full width of façade. Claw feet. From Saint-Jean-de-Cornac, near Moissac. Property of Mme. C. R. (Photo: L. Violle.)   *facing p.* 37

PLATE VIII

ARM-CHAIR (*Chaire à bras*), sixteenth century. *Hospice de Beaune* (Côte-d'Or). (Photo: Stevignou.)

ARM-CHAIR, Louis XIV. Wood carved and gilt. 3 feet 10½ inches high; 2 feet 3 inches wide. High, rectangular back. Downward-curving, scrolled arms. Square section baluster legs linked by cross-stretchers in the form of four volutes uniting at centre in richly carved motif. Piece and photo: *Musée des Arts Décoratifs.*   *facing p.* 44

PLATE IX

COMMODE, Regency. Marquetry decoration. 2 feet 6 inches high; 9 feet 4 inches wide. Trapezoid. Façade composed of two sets of drawers separated by uprights. Small cupboards at both sides. Tall feet. Bronze mounts, chased and gilt: pendants, drop handles, key-hole plates, shoes in form of lions' paws. Private collection. (Photo: Larousse.)   *facing p.* 45

PLATE X

ARM-CHAIR, Louis XV. Moulded wood, curved contours, 'violin' back, padded arm-rests on supports set back on side rails. Carved rose motif at each corner projection and at centre of traverses. *Musée des Arts Décoratifs.* (Photo: *Connaissance des Arts.*)   *facing p.* 56

PLATE XI

BUFFET, Louis XV. Regional (Normandy?). Solid oak. Full height: 8 feet 1½ inches; upper section: 5 feet 1½ inches high; 4 feet 9½ inches wide. Depth: upper section: 1 foot 1½ inches; lower section: 2 feet. Four doors with moulded panels. Ironwork decoration. Paris, property of Mme Locquin. (Photo: Larousse.)   *facing p.* 64

PLATE XII

COIFFEUSE, Louis XV. 2 feet 8 inches high; 3 feet wide; 2 feet deep. Polychrome marquetry: branches of leaves, flowers and small ornaments shown in perspective. Curved contours. Table-top opens up to reveal box compartments. Four drawers, one false drawer and pull-out-flap. Cabriole legs. Bronze mounts, chased and gilt; Rococo pendants, keyhole plates, handles and shoes. Stamped: Pierre Roussel. Private collection. (Photo: Larousse.)   *facing p.* 65

Greek-keys; pendants, surrounds and base decorated with Greek-fret
design. Stamped: J. F. Oeben. S.A.R.L. collection. Bensimon.
(Photo: Larousse.) *facing p.* 93

PLATE XX

BUREAU (*Bureau à gradin*), Louis XVI. 4 feet high; 5 feet 3 inches
wide; 3 feet 0½ inch deep. Mahogany. Rectilinear; one drawer and
two doors in front face; additional tier at back surmounted by gallery;
eight tapered pedestal legs. Bronze mounts, chased and gilt; fretwork
motifs of cornucopiae, vases of flowers and rosettes; panel surrounds
decorated with finely chased steel plaques; shoes in the form of leaves.
Stamped: J. H. Riesener. Property of M. Seligmann. (Photo:
Larousse.) *facing p.* 96

PLATE XXI

BONHEUR-DU-JOUR, Louis XVI. 3 feet 8 inches high; 2 feet 4 inches
wide; 1 foot deep. Amboyna wood. Doucine-moulded additional tier
at back containing one small cupboard compartment; one drawer in
frieze; fluted baluster legs; shelf joins legs. Bronze mounts, chased and
gilt: colonnettes on top section bulbous and fluted; borders in finely
chased steel; pearl beading, shoes. Stamped: Weisweiler. S.C.
collection. (Photo: Larousse.) *facing p.* 97

PLATE XXII

ARMOIRE, Louis XV. Tulipwood. Doors overlaid with panels of
Chinese lacquer, vermilion ground and black surround. 5 feet
7 inches high; 4 feet 8 inches wide; 1 foot 4 inches deep. Decoration
consists of small figures, palaces and trees painted in gold and black.
Sides: floral marquetry in cross-grained wood. Bronze mounts,
chased and gilt, attributed to Gouthière. Stamped: BVRB (Bernard
Van Risen Burg). *Ancienne Collection Patron. Musée du Louvre.* (Photo:
Connaissances des Arts.) *facing p.* 104

PLATE XXIII

COMMODE, Louis XVI. 2 feet 10½ inches high; 4 feet 0½ inch wide;
1 foot 10½ inches deep. Mahogany. Two drawers surmounted by one
row of three smaller drawers. Tapering, turned legs; brass: narrow
moulded border around drawers, square drop handles. Property of
Mme Locquin. (Photo: Larousse.) *facing p.* 112

PLATE XXIV

CHAIR, Consulate period. 3 feet high; 1 foot 6 inches deep. Solid
mahogany; back with pierced splat in form of broadly splayed lotus
flower surmounting a carved X in square frame; front legs baluster-
shaped, rear legs Etruscan style. Stamped: Jacob D., *rue Meslée.*
Bibliothèque Marmottan. (Photo: Larousse.)

ARM-CHAIR, Consulate period. Back with upper traverse curved
slightly outwards and overlaid with painted paper strip representing
a classical scene; traverse across middle of back pierced and carved
into five palmettes; arm-supports in form of dolphins. Front legs
turned and tapered, rear legs Etruscan style. *Bibliothèque Marmottan.*
(Photo: Larousse.) *facing p.* 113

PLATE XXV

DROP-FRONT SECRETAIRE. Marquetry of flowers and birds. Rococo-
style bronze mounts, chased and gilt: pendants, shoes, surrounds.
Stamped: Dubois. (Photo: *Connaissance des Arts.*) *facing p.* 120

the City of Paris as a gift to welcome King Charles X in 1830. Marquetry pattern on table-top: a wreath of flowers encircling a rosette formed by six lilies. Frieze: pattern of foliated scroll-work and palmettes alternated with rosettes. Legs in form of six lyres resting on hexagonal base. Stamped: Louis-François Puteaux. *Musée Carnavalet.* (Photo: Larousse.) *facing p.* 156

PLATE XXXIV

GUÉRIDON TABLE, Louis-Philippe period. 2 feet 7 inches high; diameter: 3 feet 6 inches. Mahogany. Heavy top supported by central pedestal of reeded, bulbous shape, resting on a square base, in turn supported by claw feet. Property of Mme Locquin. (Photo: Larousse.) *facing p.* 157

PLATE XXXV

BED, Second Empire. 6 feet long; 5 feet wide. Pearwood dyed black. Brass and pewter accessories and marquetry in the Boulle manner; manufactured by J. Allard (1869); modern draperies selected by Jean Pascard. *Préfecture de Grenoble.* (Photo: *Connaissance des Arts.*) *facing p.* 168

PLATE XXXVI

JEWEL CABINET, Second Empire. 3 feet 10 inches high; 3 feet 5 inches wide. Purplewood inlaid with porcelain flowers, cut out and realistically painted by Guérou. Bronze mounts, chased and gilt. Belonged at one time to the Empress Eugénie. Manufactured by Charon Frères. Property of MM. Fabius Frères. (Photo: Millet – *Connaissance des Arts.*) *facing p.* 176

PLATE XXXVII

ARM-CHAIR, Second Empire. 3 feet 8 inches high. Gilt wood. Heavily curved contours; raised and padded arm-rests; slightly cabriole legs decorated with acanthus leaves and mounted on castors. Jeanselme's freely adapted copy of a model executed by Foliot in 1774 for the *Cabinet de la Pendule* at Versailles. Upholstery in Beauvais tapestry, from the design by Chabal-Bussurgey. On display at the 1867 Exhibition. *Palais de Compiègne.* (Photo: Hutin.)

OCCASIONAL CHAIR, Second Empire. 2 feet 10 inches high. Black wood, varnished and decorated with flakes of mother-of-pearl (*burgauté*). Pierced back. *Palais de Compiègne.* (Photo: Hutin.)

CONFIDANT, Napoleon III. 2 feet 3 inches; 4 feet wide; 2 feet 5 inches deep. Gilt wood with yellow damask upholstery. Fringe trimming. *Palais de Compiègne.* (Photo: Hutin.) *facing p.* 177

PLATE XXXVIII

GUÉRIDON TABLE, Tamarind mahogany, varnished, gilt bronze mounts. Upturned trefoil top, resting on three console legs decorated with mounts representing water-lily stems. Executed by Louis Majorelle in 1902. Piece and photo: *Musée des Arts Décoratifs.* *facing p.* 192

PLATE XXXIX

SIDEBOARD (*Buffet*), 1955. 4 feet 8 inches high; 12 feet 4 inches wide; 1 foot 6 inches deep. Sliding doors in grey enamelled glass. Top in black Formica. Sides in varnished pearwood. Base supports in natural aluminium. Jacques Dumont, interior designer. (Photo: Racroul.) *facing p.* 193

JACKET

CABINET, *c.* 1670. 7 feet 6 inches high; 5 feet 6 inches wide; 1 foot 3 inches deep. Two doors, 6 feet linked in pairs by two X-shaped traverses surmounted at intersections by perfume-burners; two drawers in frieze. Marquetry in contrasting wood and ivory on ground of ebony and wood gilt. *Musée des Arts Décoratifs.* (Photo: Daunizeau.)

IN THE TEXT

TRANSLATOR'S ACKNOWLEDGEMENTS

I am extremely grateful for the invaluable help and advice given to me by Mr. L. Russell Muirhead, Mr. Francis Watson, Dr. and Mrs. Peter Murray and Mr. Michael Sternfeldt.

H. P.

| TECHNICAL INTRODUCTION

The following few pages are intended to familiarise the reader with terminology peculiar to the art of furniture-making. If we want to appreciate the true value of an *objet d'art* or to be able to describe it in clear, precise terms, it is essential we should at least have some slight knowledge of the materials used and the technical processes adopted.

1 | Manufacture

Of all the materials that artisans have had recourse to throughout the centuries in furniture-making, wood has always taken pride of place.

▶ *Wood*

All woods that are involved in the manufacture of furniture come under the heading of '*bois d'ébénisterie*', whether they are used in solid form or as veneers. Woods may be classified in various ways:

(1) ACCORDING TO THEIR ORIGIN. First of all we must distinguish between native and colonial woods. The native or national woods come from trees which grow on our soil. These trees develop slowly in a temperate climate and produce woods of soft colouring, a hard, close-grained texture and fibres which tend to run parallel. These woods are

generally used in solid form. Colonial or exotic woods come from the forests of Asia, Africa or America. They, on the contrary, have vivid colours and a highly figured grain. Their decorative value was appreciated as far back as the sixteenth century, and, in spite of the cost, they have been imported ever since. In the majority of cases, these woods are veneered in thin layers on a carcase of native wood. Nevertheless in the sixteenth century some furniture was made in solid ebony; in Louis XVI's reign and under the First Empire certain particularly luxurious pieces were made in solid mahogany. Since economic conditions have now changed, exotic woods are often used solid (purplewood, *avodiré*, gaboon for example). The scientific names and origins of exotic woods are well known. The Technical Centre for Tropical Forestry has drawn up a complete index, which any manufacturer can refer to, for all types of exotic woods (scientific and common name, description of the tree, appearance and texture of the wood, technical, physical, mechanical, aesthetic characteristics, uses, etc.). On the other hand, any such information concerning woods used in olden times is totally lacking. Roubo, in the eighteenth century, gives us a list of forty-eight woods used in *ébénisterie* but does not quote the scientific names. Neither are all the origins he supplies correct. Havard in the nineteenth century, in his *Dictionnaire de l'ameublement*, has no more information to offer. It is beyond the scope of this little book to set out all the different varieties as there are about fifty usable varieties of mahogany alone, and their origins are widespread (Ivory Coast, the Gaboon, Mexico, Cuba, etc.).

(2) According to their Technical Properties. The chief technical characteristics are: hardness, density, elasticity, toughness.

Hardness is measured by the resistance the wood fibres put up against the cutting action of the tool employed. Hard wood is difficult to work, but as compensation it generally takes polish well: oak and mahogany are cases in question.

Density. – By density we understand the quantity of solid matter contained in a given volume of wood. In order to express this density, we weigh a certain volume of wood and

1 *Cupboard, end of Twelfth Century*

compare this weight to an equal volume of water. The density of a wood is not constant; it varies according to the tree's age, the soil on which it grew, the nature of that soil, the section of tree examined, etc. Box (0·912) and ebony (1·200) have a high density and are very heavy; poplar (0·390) and pine (0·463) are light, porous woods.

Elasticity. – A wood is said to be elastic when it returns to its original shape when released from stress. Elm, spruce, larch and ash are elastic woods; oak on the other hand does not possess this property at all.

Toughness is that property which enables wood to bend without breaking. Dense woods are tougher than porous woods; elm, oak, ash and hornbeam are tough woods. The use of a wood is determined by its technical properties. In the sixteenth century walnut was favoured more than oak. Since walnut is in fact softer to work on and takes polish well, it was the wood most suited to lavish decorative carving (see Plate vi). *Menuisiers* (see Glossary) of the eighteenth century valued the elasticity of beech (see Plate x) for making chairs with curved outlines.

(3) ACCORDING TO THEIR NATURAL COLOUR. This classification applies chiefly to veneering, marquetry and inlay work. Great value can in fact be attached to a wood, either for its natural colouring or the special pattern of its grain. A marquetry-worker more than anyone else is interested in the colours of wood. Some of the white woods, barely coloured at all, are: holly, hornbeam, sycamore, service, birch. We get a yellow tint in satinwood, lime, box, tulipwood; red tones in mahogany; yellowish brown in chestnut, cherry, thuya; brown in walnut, purplewood, kingwood; black in ebony. Some veined woods offer a combination of two colours. Tulipwood for instance is pale yellow with a red vein; purplewood, known as violetwood in the seventeenth century, is the colour of white wine with a greyish brown vein; olive is deep yellow with purplish brown stripes.

The natural woods therefore offer a wide range of colours, especially as there are subtly different shades of each colour according to the species of tree. Satinwood gives us a true yellow, lime a pale yellow, and tulipwood a yellow verging almost on green. Some colours though, are missing altogether, true green and blue for instance. In these cases we are forced to use dyes. Dyeing wood is an age-old practice. Ever since the sixteenth century French artisans have done as the Italians of the Quattrocento did and made imitations of costly woods by means of dyes: pear dyed black is a substitute for ebony. By the eighteenth century dyeing wood was common practice in marquetry. Nevertheless, despite Roubo, we have little or no information concerning either methods or dyes. Each master jealously guarded his trade secrets. At the beginning of the nineteenth century wood-dyeing was widely adopted in order to dispense with the excessive cost of importation. In 1801, in his *Annales du Musée,* Landon advised the use of native woods and sets out formulae for dyeing them. Wood dyes are a specialised industry today.

Not all woods take dye well. All periods and all *ébénistes* have their favourite woods. We need only say that hornbeam, holly, sycamore, maple and pear (for black) have often been used. There is also a wide variety of dyes. The natural ones listed by Roubo (indigo for blue, weld for yellow, arnatto for red, campeachy for purple etc.), are generally replaced now by chemical dyes (nitric, sulphuric, hydrochloric, oxalic acid). Originally each wood was dyed by a different process and it was these processes, varying with each master, that rendered the dye fast or otherwise in the wood. In any case, as far as marquetry is concerned, natural woods are preferable to artificially coloured ones. Veined woods are highly prized, especially for veneering. Some trees tend to produce woods where the grain follows a certain distinctive pattern. We should also consider the varieties of wavy-grained woods – where the more or less regular grain is divided up into different shades of colour like waves; woods with roe or 'watered' figures – where the grain echoes the fancy pattern of *moiré* silk fabrics; woods with flame-like markings – where the swirly, highly figured grain, in sheaf-like formation, simulates flames; strongly dotted figures, fiddle-back figures or spotted figures – where the grain shows the attractive effect of small, closely packed round or oval knots, either lighter or darker than the background; 'twisted' grain woods – where we find an interlocking grain surrounding plain, irregularly scattered areas; curl figures (see Plate xxvi) which come from the stump of the tree and produce oddly assorted patterns in rich colours. We may also mention those woods with looping, feathery (i.e. Cuba curl), mottled, ribboned, birds-eye and striated grains.

Of all the different types of wood, mahogany has perhaps the most interesting and varied grain. As early as the end of the eighteenth century *ébénistes* (see Glossary) made good use of its peculiarities for veneers covering a large surface area. As mahogany was so expensive, artisans started searching at the beginning of the nineteenth century for native woods which might provide the same decorative interest: plane, beech, thuya, yew, ash and maple were already used during the Empire and their distinctive grain was often to be seen in the Restoration period.

Special attention should be accorded to burrs. Burrs are excrescences found on certain trees; they are caused by various phenomena; insect bites, breakages and parasitic plants; all these damage the *liber* and cause the sap to collect at certain points. Small leaves of veneer may be taken from these burrs but they vary in appearance; flowery patterns twist and twine in minute rays and spread out in fan-like formation around a multitude of knots; amboyna, thuya, ash (see Plate xxxiii), elm and walnut are liable to produce burrs. Burrs as veneers are a fairly recent innovation in the art of furniture-making; the first examples date from the Empire; they were frequently used during the Restoration.

Thus we find that this basic, unique material, wood, is very versatile. Furniture-makers have shown a preference for this or that species according to period or fashion. Naturally, the sixteenth-century *menuisier* could not have recourse to the infinite variety of woods that we have today; yet at all periods artists have been faced with the subtle and complex problem of choosing a wood. In fact their success or failure depends above all on their wise choice of a basic material.

▶ *Woodwork : Joints*

The earliest pieces of furniture were made simply by placing extremely thick planks of wood side by side: a wrought-iron band held the different panels together and made certain that such furniture was strongly secured (see Chap. II, p. 48). From the end of the thirteenth century onwards this rudimentary process was abandoned and the first joints were invented (see Chap. II, p. 49). After that *menuisiers* never ceased to experiment with new combinations whereby they might achieve both strength and elegance. From the eighteenth century onwards the *menuisier* had a great variety of joints at his disposal: the introduction of machine tools in mid-nineteenth century only meant that the different joints were assembled at greater speed, but as often as not they were also weaker. We can count about forty types of joints, some crude, others refined, some ingenious and others impractical. Here we will merely describe the commonest ones.

(1) MORTISE-AND-TENON JOINT. The object of this joint is to join two pieces of wood together at a right angle. A tenon – in other words a rectangular projection at the end of one member, cut with the grain – is fitted into a cavity of exactly the same dimensions, called a mortise. This cavity has likewise been cut with the grain, but hollowed out in that side of the second member which is to be jointed to the first.

The tenon should not pass right through the adjoining member: it should be stopped by a shoulder, thus making the joint neater and stronger.

(2) OPEN TENON JOINT. Here the tenon is the same width as the member of which it forms part, and the same length as the width of the second member. A socket is cut right across the end of the second member; the resulting shape reminds us of the prongs of a fork, hence the French name of this joint – *enfourchement*.

These two joints can only be made strong in wood where the grain runs straight: i.e. lengthwise parallel fibres are the only ones which give a strong mortise and tenon.

For woods that have to be bent (those in Louis XV chairs for example) we use the following:

(3) DOWEL JOINT. Dowels are small cylinders of wood. They should be used only on narrow, thin pieces of wood, since they do not make for a very accurate or strong joint. Two or three dowelling pins usually take the place of a tenon.

Both members are bored so that the holes meet; the dowelling pins are then driven in and glued.

(4) DOVETAIL OR SWALLOW-TAIL JOINT. Used chiefly to joint two relatively broad, thin members at an angle. This joint was frequently employed on chests and nowadays serves for drawers. Several trapezoid projections – called tenons or male tails – are fitted into sockets – mortises or female tails – of the same shape and size, cut out of the adjoining member. The trapezoid shape reminds us of a swallow's tail, hence the French name *queue d'hironde* (swallow-tail) which has been corrupted into *queue d'aronde*.

(5) CONCEALED JOINT. When the joint must not show too obviously on the surface of the two members, 'concealed' or 'covered' joints are used: a thin layer of wood on the outer surfaces of each member is left uncut. In this way the tenons are hidden secretly in the thickness of the wood.

(6) TONGUE-AND-GROOVE JOINT. This joint is generally used in two instances: when members have to be jointed lengthwise in order to form panels that are wider than the planks available; when panels have to be jointed into frames. This joint is made by a combination which goes under the name of joggle or tongue-and-groove. The tongue is a kind of continuous tenon, cut along the full length of one member; the groove is a kind of mortise formed by a channel in the lengthwise section, hollowed out along the full length of the adjoining member. When there is only one groove it is called a simple tongue-and-groove; when there are two it is double.

(7) MITRE JOINT. This is a joint serving to unite two members at an angle of 45°, thus forming a frame. It is more refined than the square-cut mortise and tenon, since the grain of the wood and the elaborate shape of the mouldings can be matched exactly along a line bisecting the angle formed by the two members. It can be made in the form of a mortise and tenon, tongue-and-groove or open tenon.

▶ *Secondary Materials (bronze, iron, silver, plastic)*

We will just mention briefly that in some exceptional cases

materials other than wood have been used for furniture, but we will not go into the manufacturing processes in detail.

The Dagobert throne and the Bayeux arm-chair are cases in point, the first being made of gilt bronze and the second in wrought-iron (see Chap. II, p. 45). To satisfy their monarch's whim, goldsmiths in the seventeenth century manufactured orange-tree tubs, tables and candelabra in solid *silver* for Versailles (see Chap. V, p. 88).

At the end of the eighteenth century and under the Empire, some pieces were made entirely out of iron and bronze in an attempt to copy the metal furniture discovered at Herculaneum and Pompeii, notably those types of tripod called *athéniennes* (see Chap. VII, p. 128). Under the Second Empire (see Chap. X, p. 176) one curious process was to use *papier mâché* lacquered black for the backs of certain chairs.

Basket-work, which had been known since the Louis XIII period, became highly fashionable in the Second Empire and is still commonly used nowadays, particularly for garden furniture.

Lastly, among the most modern materials, we should note plastics, moulded wood and metal tubing.

2 | Decoration

No article of furniture, however humble, comes to us utterly deprived of decorative elements. This decoration gives rise to a tremendous variety of processes and materials. The only decoration on the earliest pieces of furniture consisted of a network of wrought-iron bands. As far as the medieval *menuisiers* were concerned, strap-hinges and iron fittings had first and foremost a utilitarian function. The decorative effect was achieved almost by accident, unconsciously.

Carving appears on furniture from the thirteenth century onwards. This solid wood carving is at all times the sole ornamentation for furniture in daily use (see Plate xi).

Work in solid wood brings us to three technical processes: moulding, turning, decorative carving.

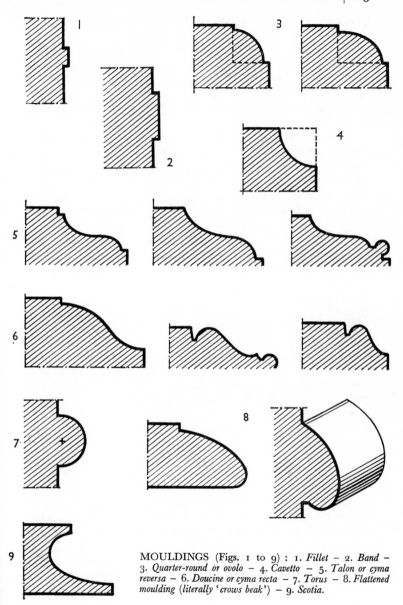

MOULDINGS (Figs. 1 to 9) : 1. *Fillet* – 2. *Band* –
3. *Quarter-round or ovolo* – 4. *Cavetto* – 5. *Talon or cyma
reversa* – 6. *Doucine or cyma recta* – 7. *Torus* – 8. *Flattened
moulding (literally 'crows beak')* – 9. *Scotia.*

▶ *Moulding*

All projections, round or square, curved or straight, which serve to decorate a piece of furniture are called mouldings. Mouldings are used to accentuate the general structure of furniture. The following are various types:

(*a*) *Flat* mouldings: fillet or listel (Fig. 1), band or plat-band (Fig. 2);

(*b*) *Curved* mouldings: quarter-round (Fig. 3) also called echinus, ovolo or egg-and-dart, cavetto or *congé* (Fig. 4), talon (Fig 5), doucine (Fig. 6), torus (Fig. 7), flattened moulding (Fig. 8), scotia (Fig. 9);

(*c*) *Mixed* or *composite* mouldings made up of several types.

As the combinations of the different mouldings are infinite, we can obtain a great many profiles.

Mouldings are not usually left bare; they are enriched with ornamentation, some of the commonest forms being the acanthus leaf (Fig. 11), waterlily leaf (Fig. 12), *raies de coeur* (Fig. 13), wave-band (Fig. 14), Greek key (Fig. 15), gadrooning, imbricated scalework (Fig. 16), interlaced designs (Fig. 17), ribbon mouldings (Figs. 18, 19, 20), pearl beading (Fig. 21), egg-and-darts. Moulding varies in richness according to period. It already occupies an important place in Renaissance decoration, but never does it play a more important role than in the reign of Louis XIII: then it no longer stops at accentuating the architectural form of a piece of furniture but spreads into the panels as well (see Chap. IV, p. 74 and Plate VI).

Empire furniture, on the other hand, is almost totally devoid of mouldings.

▶ *Turning*

This is a carved moulding, executed on a lathe. It was an extraordinarily popular method of decoration in the reign of Louis XIII. Every possible combination was devised by the *menuisiers* of that time (see Chap. IV, p. 73). Turning came back into favour with the imitation Louis XIII style at the end of the nineteenth century under the Second Empire.

III *Buffet, c. 1580*

▶ *Carving*

The panel to be decorated with a carved motif is first clamped to the work-bench and then the general outline of the decoration, that part to be removed from the solid block, is drawn on the smooth surface. The carver's tools consist of:

(1) Tools for cutting (gouge, burin);
(2) Tools for modelling concave or convex surfaces (planes);
(3) Dividers (inside and outside calipers) for measuring dimensions accurately.

In most cases low relief carving is used on furniture. If the carving is particularly shallow it is executed in very low relief or, as it is called, flat carving (see Chap. IV, p. 78). Alternatively, it can be executed in high relief: the mythical figures and chimeras which adorn the uprights of Renaissance and Empire furniture jut out from the general plumb of the piece, but they are still an integral part of the upright. We come lastly to furniture with figures carved in the round, in other words, full relief. Under the Empire, the chimeras become completely detached from the carcase or serve as legs for tables or *guéridons*; these are carved in the round. Low relief carving conforms to the rules for ornamentation laid down in each period. The medieval *huchier* carves ogees whereas the sixteenth-century *menuisier* carves grotesque and allegorical figures. In the seventeenth and eighteenth centuries, carving disappears almost entirely from the panels of furniture. It retreats to the friezes and legs of tables, though it is also still used to decorate wooden seats and beds. Under Louis XIV, favourite motifs were lozenges enclosing small blossoms, acanthus leaves, masks with coronas; under Louis XV, *rocaille* and floral motifs; under Louis XVI and the Empire, classical ornaments. The Second Empire sees an exuberant decorative carving restored to its place of honour, overburdening

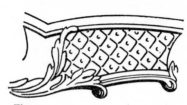

Fig. 10

Lozenge pattern enclosing small blossoms

table- and chair-legs and once more invading panels. Carving plays an important part in furniture decoration right until the First World War.

► *Inlay-work*

The three different processes of inlay-work, veneering and marquetry are often confused since all three have the common purpose of decorating furniture (where the carcase is in native wood of little value) by the application of precious materials (exotic woods, metals, etc.).

Inlay-work appears to be the oldest of these processes. The artist chisels out the base-wood to a certain depth in a given pattern; he also cuts thin strips from one or more different materials to exactly the same size and shape of the interstices made in the carcase. He then inserts the strips he has cut into these cavities, where they are held fast by a drop of glue. This kind of work not only applies to wood: it is also used on metal and in such cases it is called damascening.

The materials employed for inlays are immensely varied. During the Renaissance, when the imitation Italian style was current, inlays were made of precious stones (jasper, lapis lazuli), metals (brass, pewter, silver) and animal products (tortoise-shell, mother-of-pearl, ivory). Even coloured mastics were used. This technique remained in fashion for luxury articles all through the seventeenth century. In the eighteenth century *ébénistes* inlaid narrow fillets of exotic, coloured woods in a frame round the marquetry design; alternatively, the inlay was of the same kind of wood but with the grain running in a different direction. Veneers and marquetry are cut with the grain; inlays across the grain. The Directory, and later the Empire, see the use of exotic wood inlays with very bold contrasts of colour (satinwood on ebony for example). The Restoration and Second Empire remain faithful to this technique but with variations in materials; ebony and mother-of-pearl are frequently employed.

► *Veneering*

With the remaining two processes – veneering and marquetry

– the base-wood is not incised at all; the decoration is applied by glueing it directly on to the foundation carcase.

The carcase will probably be in native wood; oak constitutes an excellent carcase since it is very strong and takes glue well, but many pieces of veneered furniture are made in wood of a far inferior quality, such as poplar and pine.

The carcase has to be prepared. The panels for veneering are scored with a tooth-plane. The plane-iron is cross-hatched, in other words, closely spaced parallel ridges run both lengthwise and across the iron. The cutting edge is composed of a number of small teeth that scratch the wood, thus levelling the surface and covering it with striae or criss-cross lines which are a great help in making the wood absorb the glue.

In about 1840 a new process was introduced on high-class furniture: laminated veneers. A preliminary veneer, generally an exotic wood – tulipwood for example – is inserted immediately on top of the carcase; the preliminary veneer is laid across the grain and this thin layer of wood, where the grain runs in an opposite direction to that of the carcase and the face veneer, keeps the top decorative layer very firmly in place.

Veneer was not always cut in the same way; decorative effects varied according to the methods used: The *ébénistes* of old only had a hand-saw and could not cut the layers thinner than 2·5 mm. They sawed the wood in three different ways:

(*a*) Down the length of the tree-trunk: the wood fibres retain their even, parallel grain.

(*b*) Obliquely, into flitches: the veins show an elliptical formation.

(*c*) At right angles to the grain: the veins show a circular, rose formation.

Nowadays, with the aid of highly developed machine tools, wood is sawn, sliced or rotary cut.

Mechanically saw-cut veneers are definitely thinner than the veneers of old. The advantage of this process is that the full richness of the wood's natural colour is preserved.

Flat-sliced veneers are not so good to work with – their colours are paler. This process is carried out by passing the

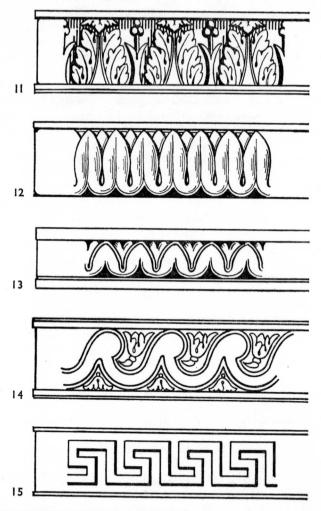

ORNAMENTATION AND MOULDINGS (Figs. 11 to 15) : 11. *Acanthus leaf* – 12. *Waterlily leaf* – 13. *Raies de coeur* – 14. *Vitruvian scroll or wave-band* – 15. Greek key.

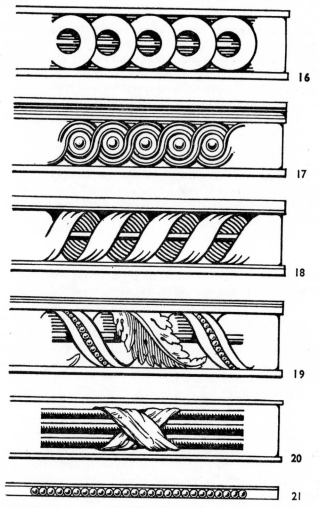

ORNAMENTATION AND MOULDINGS (Figs. 16 to 21) : 16. *Piastre or imbricated scalework* – 17. *Entrelacs or interlacing moulding* – 18. *Ribbon design* – 19. *Ribbon design interlaced with oak leaves* – 20. *Ribbon knot* – 21. *Pearl beading.*

wood under a steam-jet and then slicing it with a knife to separate the wood fibres.

Rotary-cut veneers are very interesting; by this method large areas of veneer can literally be peeled off the log; it also avoids the necessity for joints that would break up the unity of the veneered surface. Veneers of this kind are obtained with a band saw which saws off layers from a given section of the tree-trunk in a direction parallel to the fibres of the concentric rings, with the result that the colouring shows no sudden changes.

Veneering is a process which makes it possible to use woods that are interesting from a decorative point of view, but whose small size (i.e. burls), whose resistance to cutting (woods with a twisted grain difficult to work, i.e. yew), or whose limited availability (i.e. purplewood) preclude their being used in solid form for furniture.

▶ *Crossbanding*

Carcases may be decorated by simply applying a single sheet of veneer that has no particular decorative value but is large enough to cover the whole area of a panel. In such cases strongly dotted or curly-grained woods are often used.

Panels can, however, be decorated with small pieces of veneer fitted together in such a way that the grain changes direction and thus also changes tone according to the light. This is called crossbanding.

In this event the panel is usually surrounded by a band of veneer, called a border, that forms a frame and matches at the corners.

There are many different combinations. The simplest crossbanding comprises four pieces of veneer cut so that the grain matches at the joints, forming a cross, + or ×. Diamond-point veneers require the grain of each piece to run parallel with the frame and to match along the diagonals of the panel. Fan-shapes, sunbursts, etc. are also used in crossbanding.

For the usual type of pattern, we choose veneers of even grain which have been cut out in adjacent strips, so that when the whole panel is made up, the same shadings mirror each other along the joints. In simple designs the effect may be varied by the use of woods with leaf or branch patterns in the figure (curl or flame-like figures) or those sliced in flitches. Thus, when the pieces of veneer are cut to match symmetrically, they form a kind of rosette.

▶ *Parquetry*

Veneers made up of small strips cut from the same piece of wood and arranged in more elaborate geometrical patterns are called parquetry designs. These small strips of veneer are fitted together to cover the whole area of the panel to be decorated (their grain running in opposite directions); the variations in tone obtained are entirely different from those obtained from a single, unbroken, sheet of veneer. Woods of varying colours can also be mixed to obtain a polychrome parquetry.

As with crossbanding, there are an almost infinite number of geometrical combinations (see Plate xix). The commonest are squares, arranged in draughtboard, diamond patterns or lozenges with the grain in opposite directions. Some of the rarer ones are stars, composed of triangles, mosaics of cubes and imitation basket-work.

Parquetry marks the borderline between the process called veneering and that called marquetry. In all the combinations we have just described (large area veneers, crossbanding, parquetry) the strips of veneer used have *straight edges* and may easily be cut and adjusted to the right size with an *ébéniste's* standard tools. This is not so for veneers with *curved outlines* because these require a *marquetry saw*.

▶ *Marquetry*

We can distinguish between marquetry and veneering because marquetry necessitates the drawing of a *design*. A few simple guide-marks on the carcase are all that is needed for veneering, even for parquetry, since this work is absolutely regular and repetitive; nevertheless some of the more complicated parquetry patterns are treated in the same manner as marquetry.

Marquetry calls for a series of long and delicate operations.

(1) MARKING OUT A PATTERN. An *ébéniste* may choose to make use of a design by an *ornemaniste* or *dessinateur*; he may also devise his own decorative motif. There are two processes by which he can reproduce the design on the wood carcase: (*a*) he traces the design straight on to the wood panel. In order to speed up this preliminary operation, some eighteenth century *ébénistes* kept ready-cut master patterns in brass or iron; (*b*) he can also quite simply take a paper pattern with the design traced on it and stick it on to the wood direct.

(2) CUTTING OUT THE VENEER. The thin sheets of wood ready for veneering are carefully sorted out according to their colour and grain. Next the *ébéniste* cuts out small strips exactly conforming to the design, as regards both colour and shape.

In the sixteenth and seventeenth centuries the cutting out was done with a burin and not a marquetry saw; the narrow strips were therefore often splintered at the edges. The procedure is, however, slightly different for marquetry in ebony, brass, pewter, tortoiseshell or ivory, as we know it was uniquely practised by J.-C. Boulle and his imitators. Two sheets of material (ivory and ebony for example), of absolutely identical thickness, are glued together, one on top of the other. A piece of paper with the design drawn on it is stuck on top of the two sheets and the pattern is cut out with a burin or a saw. After they have been cut, the layers of ivory and ebony are taken apart and it is then possible to decorate two panels of the same size with a marquetry design that is similar, but not identical, i.e. in one the background is ebony (this is *première partie* marquetry), and in the other the background is ivory (*deuxième partie* marquetry).

(3) ASSEMBLING THE PIECES OF THE PATTERN. The contrasting pieces that will comprise the finished pattern are reassembled and fitted together on a backing of thin material or a sheet of paper; they are stuck face downwards on to the material, i.e. on the side that will show when the piece of furniture is completed.

(4) GLUEING THE CARCASE. Whether it is veneer or marquetry that the *ébéniste* has prepared, both are fixed on to

IV *Buffet, Renaissance*

the carcase in the same manner. The panel is coated with glue. The holding power of the veneer depends largely on the quality of glue and the secrets of mixing glue have always been jealously guarded by each workshop. In the eighteenth century special use was made of a good strong glue called *colle d'Angleterre*. Glues in any case were made from nerve fibre, skin and bone, and are known today as Givet or Lyon glue. Glue must be laid on very thick and very hot. It must be spread evenly and the water content must not be altered once glueing operations have begun. Synthetic glues have recently been introduced and the advantage of these is that they can be applied cold; they contain a base of phenol, urea, and formol, or a base of cellulose derivatives melted down in solvents like acetone, amyl acetate, benzine or alcohol. Synthetic resins are also used for glue.

Fixing the Marquetry Design on to the Carcase. This operation must be done very quickly; the *ébéniste* takes a marquetry iron which he keeps hot and a marquetry hammer; the point of this hammer is exceptionally wide, its edges are blunted and it is set at an angle, sloping backwards towards the handle. With the aid of these two instruments, the *ébéniste* presses the marquetry down hard on to the carcase. In most cases adhesion is assured by means of cauls, in other words, presses with big boards of mahogany, zinc or cardboard. For surfaces which need to be bent, curved cauls are used, but for other graceful shapes for which cauls cannot be made, *ébénistes* use sacks of sand that will mould into the required shape. For turned shapes he uses circular bands.

The hot process, which is noxious for the worker, is hardly ever used now since modern glues can be applied cold.

(6) Levelling off. The cloth is removed, clinging threads are pulled away and any glue that has oozed out is removed with a chisel or wooden spatula. When the marquetry is quite dry, the panel is levelled off with a tooth-plane and then it is ready for polishing.

▶ *Furniture Finishes: Polishing, Varnishing*

Both solid furniture and furniture covered with marquetry

v *Table, Sixteenth Century*

c

must be given extremely careful polishing before being delivered to the client. This polishing will bring out the natural beauty of the veins and colouring.

We begin by removing any roughness with a rasp, then we rub it down with pumice-stone, either dry or moistened with oil or water. Next comes the real polishing, with sand paper, scouring-rush and, finally, rottenstone. Only when the surface of the furniture is perfectly smooth can we put on varnish or beeswax.

Varnish preserves the gloss on a polished surface; it safeguards the furniture from dryness, humidity, insects and mildew.

The ingredients of varnish vary a great deal. In general they are resinous substances, transparent, soluble in alcohol or turpentine and are applied in thin coats. In olden times varnishes contained a base of certain oils which tended to dry up and lose their fatty essence.

Solid wood furniture is often polished with a good yellow wax melted down in turpentine.

In recent years furniture manufacturers have devised a new process of sanding and white-leading solid wood. This process consists in filling up the pores of certain woods, notably oak, with hard substances whose colour contrasts with the wood base.

All the processes we have so far described – moulding, turning, carving, inlay-work, veneering, marquetry – achieve their decorative effect by virtue of the wood itself. We will now examine those decorative processes which involve other materials besides wood: paint, lacquer, bronze.

▶ *Painting and Gilding Wood*

Certain pieces of furniture have always been painted. We shall see later on that most furniture of the Middle Ages seems to have been painted (see Chap. II, p. 47); this we can guess from a few traces of colour still visible and from pictures of the original pieces left by church carvers.

In the seventeenth and eighteenth centuries the majority of wooden seats and beds were gilt or painted in a wide variety of colours – blue, sea-green, grey. The search for polychrome effects led painters to make the carvings and mouldings a different colour from the background : hence we find blue on a white ground, jonquil yellow on pale green, blue on pale yellow, etc. Yet another method used was that of painting in contrasting tones, i.e. picking out the mouldings and carving in pale colours against a background of the same colour but deeper in tone.

Apart from this, we seldom find painting on furniture during the seventeenth and eighteenth centuries, though it is true that tables and consoles are often gilt. Usually, however, colour in decoration is achieved by other methods (veneering, marquetry, lacquer, porcelain). We have to wait for a dearth of inspiration such as the Directory before furniture-makers are satisfied merely to paint the wood.

The old-fashioned processes, which were intricate and lengthy because each coat had to dry out thoroughly before the next could be applied, were described in 1772 by the *peintre-doreur* Watin. We are obliged to turn to him, as we are to Roubo for woodwork, to get any idea of the methods adopted long ago.

(1) SIZE-COLOURING. The wood is covered with a layer of *glue* which is a gelatinous mixture cleverly made from skins boiled together, stock of garlic and absinthe, with salt and vinegar added. Several coats are necessary (four to eight). Next the wood is treated with a primer of whiting and hot glue. We rub it down with a pumice-stone moistened in cold water, taking great care to reach into all the small hollows of the carvings and mouldings; only then can we proceed to apply the powdered colour, mixed with glue. We finish by brushing over the whole with a very weak, transparent glue. All that remains is to varnish it.

(2) OIL-COLOURING. We lay on an undercoat (very fine lead whiting mixed with linseed oil) and cover this with a layer of *teinte dure* (white lead ground into thick oil). After *pumicing* we apply three coats of the chosen colour (oil colours diluted with turpentine). We finish with a coat of varnish.

As with painting, gilding wood is done by two different processes.

(1) WATER GILDING. The wood is coated with glue and primed in the same way as for size-colouring; we then degrease the wood and rub it down with a scouring-rush; we tint it yellow with a yellow ochre dye, diluted with skin glue. Then we put on the foundation (usually three coats), which is a mixture of Armenian bolus ground, plumbago and olive oil and makes a hard, smooth base. After that we apply the gold leaf by the simple expedient of clean, cold water.

(2) OIL GILDING. There is no undercoat this time; it is replaced by a compound gold size – a thick glutinous mixture made up from old remains of powdered gold ground into oil.

The gilt surface is burnished with an *agate* burnisher and thus takes on the required shine and glitter.

▶ *Lacquer and Varnish*

The first panels of lacquer that were used in the seventeenth century to decorate furniture were imported from the Far East. French *vernisseurs* were soon induced by the very high cost price of these panels to try and penetrate the manufacturing secrets. Although they were never able to equal the oriental lacquers for durability or brilliance, French artisans of the mid-eighteenth century did manage to achieve a faithful imitation of the Chinese and Japanese lacquers. These lacquers, inspired by the designs of artists like Boucher or Pillement, were in perfect harmony with the decorative trends of the Louis XV period (see Chap. VI, p. 106). Watin, *peintre, doreur et marchand de couleurs*, produced a work entitled *L'art de faire et d'employer des vernis ou l'art du vernisseur* published in 1772, in which he records the complex researches undertaken by the *vernisseurs*, notably the Martin brothers, in an effort to equal the Far Eastern models.

Making a panel of lacquer is always a long and laborious task; the processes vary enormously but the basic operations are practically always the same. We use a light, thoroughly dry, smooth wood (lime, pear, maple) as a baseboard. We stretch a piece of muslin or hemp over the wood to prevent it from slipping. Then we lay on a primer (Bougival whiting, diluted with glue and slightly warmed). We leave the coating to dry out, then rub it down with pumice-stone, scouring-

vi *Cupboard, Louis XIII*

rush and rottenstone. Next we apply numerous coats of lacquer (sometimes twenty) with a hair brush until we get a thickness varying from 2 to 3 millimetres. In the Far East this work can continue over several years.

Lacquer is a resin extracted from trees or bushes of the turpentine family. It emerges as a thick cream, pale gold, and almost colourless. This colourless resin turns black when pounded with an iron pestle in a metal vat. If we add colouring agents we get red lacquers, some with a brownish tint to them, or the more unusual ones such as yellow, green, blue and white. The French *vernisseurs* created a far wider range of colours than that used by the Far Eastern artists. Watin gives the formulae for over twenty-five different colours.

Having thus obtained a background, the artist draws his ornamental design with a very hard, fine point (wood or iron). Then he fills it in, either flat or in slight relief. Some backgrounds are *aventuriné*, meaning that they are powdered (sometimes by means of a special little sieve) with evenly spaced glittering gold spangles or flakes of mica (yellow, green, reddish brown). Lacquers are said to be *burgauté* (see Plate XXXVI) when the flakes are tiny particles of mother-of-pearl.

The highly-coloured Coromandel lacquers bring us to an entirely different process; to be accurate, these lacquers did not originate from the east coast of India. The process was invented at Peking at the end of the seventeenth century, but the first objects we find lacquered in this way were sent to France from Pondicherry by a manager of the French East India Company, hence this erroneous name which still persists.

With Coromandel lacquers, the lacquer coating is cut away in parts, right down to the wood. The part which is to form the outline of the design is left in relief, and those parts cut away are filled in with a wide assortment of other vividly coloured lacquers.

The so-called Peking lacquered furniture, on the other hand, is red. The very thick coat of lacquer is sometimes carved superficially but never cut deep enough to reveal the wood. These distinctive types of lacquer still exist.

Enamel paint (paint with a varnish base) is commonly

VII *Cupboard, Louis XIV*

used nowadays; this is a modern process which obviously has only a distant, vague connection with the old processes; it is merely a quick, cheap way of giving a piece of furniture in common wood a glossy, washable surface affording no decorative interest.

▶ *Porcelain Plaques*

We will just mention this process without detailing the technique since it really belongs to the realm of ceramic art. It was practised in the eighteenth and, for a short time, in the nineteenth centuries by some of the *ébénistes*, Carlin in particular (see Plate xxvii). Furniture artists used the works at Sèvres or the English Wedgwood factory as sources of supply for plaques which they set into panels of their furniture.

▶ *The Manufacture of Bronze Mounts*

Bronze accessories make their appearance on seventeenth-century furniture in the work of J.-C. Boulle. They are still in use even today. In order to make a bronze mount three utterly different operations are necessary: designing; moulding and casting; chasing. For the general run of bronze mounts, these operations would be carried out by one and the same craftsman, the bronze-worker. It is to him that the *ébéniste* goes to choose his pendants, handles, shoes and key-hole plates which are adapted, successfully or not as the case may be, to the piece of furniture under current construction. The models are repeated many times and often show little or no originality. In other instances, for high quality furniture, these three operations are carried out separately; the *ébéniste* in person (Oeben, for the *Bureau du Roi*) or an *orne-maniste* (Bérain, Percier) supplies the design; a *fondeur* casts the bronze and a *ciseleur* (Caffieri, Gouthière) chases the piece and brings out its full artistic merit. Some *ébénistes* who were renowned for their bronze-work on furniture executed one or more of these operations themselves (Boulle, Cressent).

More or less the same series of operations has to be carried out, whether the bronze mount is mass produced or specially designed.

Once the design has been chosen, the first stage of the work is executed by the *modeleur*. He makes a plaster or wood model exactly the same size and shape as the final bronze. This model is in fact a positive. The *fondeur* makes a sand mould. This is perfectly normal practice in founding. The hollow mould forms a negative into which molten metal is poured.

The *cire perdue* process is longer and more delicate. It is reserved for bronze mounts of exceptional artistic value, since the mould can only be used once; the piece is therefore unique. A wax model of the piece as it will finally appear in bronze is made on a fire-proof core consisting of oddly assorted materials (pounded brick, sand, charcoal, plaster mixed with cow-hide or fibre). In this case it is a tricky job indeed to make the outer mould that encases the wax model; it is composed of the same fire-proof materials as the core (see Glossary).

The metal known as art bronze used for bronze mounts on furniture is an alloy of copper, tin, zinc and lead in varying proportions. As each alloy has its advantages and dis-advantages and differs in appearance, the proportions of the alloy vary a great deal according to the period and artist.

The piece that leaves the *fondeur* is a very imperfect re-production of the original model. Disfiguring stalks of metal are left sticking out at points where the liquid metal was run into the mould; risers, blisters, drips, roughness and welding defects all play their part in making it unrecognisable. It is in this rudimentary shape that it is handed over to the *ciseleur*.

Once the bronze has been fixed in a vice, the first stage of roughing down starts with cutting tools (chisel, gouge, burin). In some cases the *ciseleur* leaves this preparatory work to an assistant, even though any flaw in execution might damage the beauty of the work for ever. Only at this point does the really artistic part of the work begin. By using scribers to carve out the reliefs and make them sharper, planishers to smooth the surface, rifflers to polish it and matting punches to give it a 'modelled' effect, the *ciseleur* transforms the shapeless lump of bronze as it emerged from casting into a work of art that bears the strong imprint of his own personality.

Bronze mounts are not fixed on to furniture as soon as they leave the *ciseleur*'s hands; they are generally gilt or given a patina.

▶ *Bronze Gilding*

The craft of the *doreur* is independent of the *fondeur-ciseleur* partnership, though the distinction between the two professions was not always recognised.

The piece as it is handed to the *doreur* by the *ciseleur* must be scrupulously cleaned before being gilt or patinated. Gold can only be applied to perfectly clean metal. The piece is therefore dipped into a bath containing a nitric or azotic acid base, and vigorously scoured with a special very hard brush; the gold may then be applied by several different processes.

(1) MERCURY GILDING: known as *or moulu*. Gold and mercury are mixed in proportions of 1 to 8 in a crucible and heated until red-hot. The amalgam is dipped in water to solidify it, clean it and remove the surplus mercury which did not mix with the gold. We then spread on the amalgam as evenly as possible with a special brush called a scratch brush and place the piece on a gilding grid under a charcoal fire. If any defects appear during the heating they can be made good by putting on more of the amalgam. After firing, we dip the piece into cold water, whereupon the mercury evaporates. If we wish to obtain a particularly fine gilt finish, we should not stop at one application. We rub over the piece with mercury or azotic acid and repeat the operation three or four times until the layer of gold is as thick as a thumb-nail.

This method of gilding turns the gold a deep yellow; it was practised all through the seventeenth and eighteenth centuries, but as the mercury fumes were harmful to the artisans' health it was abandoned shortly afterwards.

(2) MATT GILDING. This process was invented at the end of the eighteenth century, probably by the *ciseleur* Gouthière. All Empire bronze mounts were gilt by this method. We proceed at first in the same way as we did for gilding with

mercury amalgam, then we cover the piece with a mixture of salts (nitre, sea-salt, alum, potash); after that we expose it to a charcoal fire. When the mixture starts to melt and run, we quickly dip it into cold water. The salt covering immediately dissolves and the object is left with a beautiful matt gold finish.

One variation of matt gilding is nitrate gilding. This process has the advantage of being more economical on the gold.

(3) GOLD LEAF GILDING. We dip the piece into a mercury base solution, lay on the gold leaf and then heat it to make the gold stick firmly. The disadvantage of this process is that it shows where the individual pieces of gold leaf are joined together.

(4) ELECTRO-GILDING. This process was first employed for furniture bronzes at the time of Napoleon III. It enables us to obtain several shades of gold according to the composition of the metal deposit fixed by electrolysis; on the other hand, it clogs up the delicate lines made in chasing.

(5) VARNISH GILDING. This is really a feeble imitation of the proper gilding process because the liquid we brush on does not contain gold, it has a base of alcohol and coloured dyes. The disadvantage of this very tawdry kind of gilt, once it has been done, is that it soon gets tarnished.

▶ *Burnishing Gilt Bronze*

In gilding terminology, burnishing does not mean making something brown, but giving it a smooth finish and at the same time a sparkle and metallic glitter. Burnishing is therefore a matter of flattening out the roughness produced in firing. We use various tools called burnishers which in olden times were made of hematite – red or brown iron oxide – and nowadays of steel. We use a series of burnishers of varying shapes and sizes. We steep them first in vinegar and rub hard all over the gilt piece to make the gold surface smooth. Then we wash, wipe and rinse it.

BRONZE PATINA. When bronze is not gilt it is often patinated. 'Antique' green patina first came into fashion at the end of the eighteenth century in an attempt to imitate ancient furniture dug up from archaeological excavations. This simply involves brushing over the piece with a solution of sal ammoniac, brass filings and vinegar. In order to prevent the green colour going dark too quickly we wipe it with cotton-wool soaked in oil and dry it.

Some bronze is just given a brown patina. We boil a mixture of verdigris and sal ammoniac in vinegar for twenty minutes, then soak the piece to be burnished in this solution and bring it back to the boil for a quarter of an hour.

FIXING BRONZE MOUNTS. Bronze mounts are fixed on to furniture with small brass nails or round-headed wooden screws hidden in out-of-the-way places (underneath leaves etc.); they are often carelessly fitted with the screws left in evidence. Oeben appears to be the first person to attach importance to this question and he made the *fondeurs* allow for jets and pins at intervals along the back of the piece.

These spikes are given a screw-thread, knocked into the carcase and secured on the inside with a nut.

We have not devoted any space here to the modern and industrial techniques now revolutionising furniture manufacture. All the most incongruous materials are combined in modern furniture. Where wood is still used, efforts are made to speed up manufacture; thus the laborious process of fitting joints is made redundant by moulding wood to shape.

There remains only an infinitesimal number of artisans who still carry on traditional techniques; their know-how is put to its best use in restoring old furniture. Nevertheless, it is essential for us to have some knowledge of these obsolete processes if we want to appreciate the amount of ingenuity expended by the artisans of old in constantly revitalising their art, and if we want to be in a position to judge the true value of our beautiful furniture that belongs to a bygone age.

| THE MIDDLE AGES

In France the art of furniture-making developed very late. At a time when cathedrals had already been built all over France, when carvers had filled doorways and capitals with crowds of lifelike, expressive figures and illuminators had filled countless manuscripts with lavish decoration, nothing original had yet been produced in the art of woodwork.

Architecture, sculpture and painting – the major arts – are more highly developed than the decorative arts in nearly all periods of history. There will be several opportunities later on for us to see how this generalization holds good, but in this instance the reasons are more numerous and more complex.

The history of furniture is bound up with a country's social development. There has to be a certain standard of civilisation and a certain security before the climate is favourable enough for this eminently social art to flourish. How could a medieval lord possibly use a large, easily breakable piece of furniture, however rich he was? At the slightest warning he might have to move his household and quickly stow everything he possessed on to wagons. Any furniture decorated with delicate marquetry and supported on elegant, flimsy legs would never have survived the upheavals or withstood the knocks after being moved about so often. This is why the only piece of furniture in really general use is the coffer, or chest.

Another reason for this slow development might also be the fact that furniture is used by private individuals. When a cathedral is built, it is a collective piece of work: rich and poor alike collaborate in raising God's house – everyone can take pride in such an enormous work. But however magnificent a piece of furniture may be, it can only be used by one person, or at most a very limited group of people, which in the majority of cases goes no further than the family.

In short, before an artist can be encouraged to create or to try and perfect his art, he must find a clientèle. Customers in the Middle Ages were few and far between – a lord would need to be very powerfully established in order to furnish his castle. Most people lived without any furniture at all; even today in countries less civilised than France, or indeed, in the backwoods of the French countryside, it is still the general rule to have no furniture.

Social instability, private use, and lack of clientèle provide ample explanation for the scarcity of pieces manufactured in the Middle Ages, and for the difficulty we have in finding out exactly how our ancestors furnished their homes.

Not only that, but most of this furniture has disappeared. Wood is one of the least resistant materials to damage caused by the passing years, and fire, flood and transport must have made short work of those rare specimens which could have come down to us. Furthermore, we should also take deliberate destruction into account. Each generation scorns what was made in the previous age and prefers furniture in the latest fashion; naturally it is much easier to throw the old ancestral chest out of one's home and replace it with a marquetry cabinet than to replace a Gothic church door with a Renaissance façade.

We are therefore obliged to confess that our records are extremely fragmentary and apart from a few exceptional pieces jealously guarded in museums (the oldest only dates back to the last quarter of the twelfth century), we have nothing left by which we can study French furniture of the late Middle Ages.

VIII *Arm-chair, Sixteenth Century*

1 | The Oldest Known pieces of Furniture (Twelfth and Thirteenth Centuries)

▶ *The Dagobert Faldstool*

The oldest piece of furniture we have inherited is the famous Dagobert faldstool. We must at once confess that we cannot be at all sure that this is French work; neither, for more definite reasons, can we be sure that Dagobert used this chair. There has been a great deal of controversy about this key piece. Some people imagine they see in it a clumsy copy of an ancient curule chair made by St. Eloi himself; others think that in Suger's time an old folding chair was consolidated by the addition of the three pierced plaques which form the back. The latest hypothesis is that there were about 840 workshops at Saint-Denis where metal workers and goldsmiths made this faldstool for the abbot or bishop of the day. We know for a fact that the faldstool was the type of chair currently used by ecclesiastical dignitaries, kings, and, generally speaking, by all those who had to be visible to a whole assembly of people during some ceremony.

Although it was made at a later date (fourteenth century) and is much simpler, the faldstool kept in the treasury of Bayeux Cathedral echoes the same principles. We are thus almost certainly able to establish by means of illustrated documents and these two specimens that the faldstool was a noble chair in fairly common use during the Middle Ages, not manufactured by *huchiers* (chest-makers) (see Glossary) but by an entirely different guild of craftsmen, that of the goldsmiths, since it was always made in metal: the Dagobert faldstool is in gilt bronze and the one at Bayeux in wrought iron.

It is very likely that this use of metal extended to certain beds, and the construction of beds and chairs was strongly connected at other times besides the Middle Ages. In the eighteenth century for example some *menuisiers* (furniture carvers) were specialists in wooden chairs and beds. However, goldsmiths did not enter very much into the history of furniture and we will concentrate more on artisans in wood. The oldest piece of wooden furniture which we can still admire

IX *Commode, Regency*

today is the cupboard in the Church of Obazine (or Aubazine) in the Corrèze.

▶ *The Obazine Cupboard*

This cupboard (see Plate 1) almost certainly dates back to the end of the twelfth century. It appears to have been made at the same time as the church was built, since the style of the wall-cupboards still extant in the north transept is very similar. The sides have the additional decoration of shallow Romanesque arcades. The carcase consists of six very thick beams (4 inches thick, 1 foot 1 inch wide). The ends of the beams form the cupboard's feet. Wooden planks with mortise-and-tenon joints (see Chap. I, p. 20) are tailed into the framework and the whole body thus takes the form of a four-cornered box 7 feet 2 inches high, 7 feet 10 inches wide and 2 feet 8 inches deep. The front face is absolutely flat though there are two doors set into it, rounded at the top by a semicircular arch. The uprights of these doors are in fact thick enough to be tailed into one another and each door is held fast by two wrought-iron bands, called strap-hinges, and a very simply but very carefully worked bolt.

The powerful simplicity of this cupboard makes it characteristic of twelfth and even thirteenth century furniture. The wood used is oak sawn into thick, crudely trimmed planks, just as it would have been treated in general carpentry. There were no artisans then who specialised in furniture; it was still made by carpenters. At Obazine all the woodwork was probably given over to one guild regardless of whether it was general carpentry, the wall-cupboards in the transepts or the big cupboard. The joints are still rough so that additional iron fittings are needed to hold the piece together. In this case, the ironwork is simple although very carefully and attractively worked; but in the thirteenth and fourteenth centuries when strap-hinges were still used, the aim was to produce a decorative effect and the network of volutes was complicated *ad lib*. The result was often less successful in spite of the technical skill involved. The fourteenth-century cupboard door from Mont-Saint-Quentin (Somme), now in the *Musée des Arts Décoratifs* in Paris, is a good example of over-decoration in strap-hinges. The artist has draped the volutes with oak and ivy leaves and surrounded the two panels with an elaborate border which includes not only foliated scrollwork but also animal friezes (boar eating acorns, type of salamander, etc.). The strap-hinges are no more than an applied decoration arranged vertically instead of horizontally, so that they would have formed a hoop round the whole piece; they are no longer essential to hold it together; they disguise the structural form instead of accentuating it. The craftsman who fashioned the Obazine cupboard did not make this mistake and kept to an unpretentious style of decoration. The corners of the front face are rounded off by slender colonnettes cut into the solid wood; the whole is surmounted by a moulded cornice with the abacus carved in saw-tooth pattern and the sides are decorated in a restrained relief in Romanesque style.

These decorative elements have been borrowed from architecture. In every period we can see the influence of architecture on household furniture, but never again so clearly as this. In both its structure and decoration medieval furniture is like a monumental building cut down to human size.

▶ *The Bayeux and Noyon Cupboards*

These two cupboards, made at a slightly later date, have supplied us with valuable information on the manufacture of furniture in the thirteenth century, but unfortunately one is badly damaged and the other was lost in the 1914–18 war. Although we do have detailed descriptions of them, we only wish to put one fact on record here: in the Middle Ages certain pieces of furniture were painted. Those vestiges of paint which were still visible to the early historians of furniture are valuable clues for us because we can be almost certain that medieval furniture, as we now know it, was not originally lacking in decoration. Either the wood itself was painted, as was the case with the Bayeux and Moyon cupboards, or it was covered with hide or even fabric. The horse or mule skins which were glued on to the wood had the advantage of ensuring that the whole piece was tightly held together and protected against scratches when the iron strapwork was fixed on. However, bright colours and gilding must have been a short-lived fashion and the custom of painting furniture must have died out at the beginning of the fourteenth century; this would explain the almost complete dearth of specimens.

These three cupboards provide interesting evidence of an era that is practically undocumented, but we should bear in mind that these are not ordinary pieces of furniture and that they were used chiefly for religious purposes. Cupboards did not emerge as household furniture in daily use until the beginning of the eighteenth century. Up to then their purpose had been served either by chests or by cavities hewn out of the walls and closed in by doors or wood panels. In the Raoul Duseigneur room in the *Museé des Arts Décoratifs* we can see an example of linenfold wood panelling fitted with doors, and even at Blois, the Catherine de Médicis room, approximately mid-sixteenth century, contains secret cupboards built into the walls and disguised by carved panelling.

▶ *Strap-hinged Chests*

Unlike the cupboards, the two strap-hinged chests – one in the *Museé des Arts Décoratifs* and the other in the *Musée Carnavalet* – are the predecessors of a type of furniture in extremely common use for several centuries. Both of them date back to the early thirteenth century. They are similarly made in a solid, imposing fashion and consist of very thick planks of wood (6 cm. thick) with mortise-and-tenon joints, clamped together with scrolled strap-hinges. The strap-hinges are more elaborately worked than those on the Obazine cupboard, and already point to a new development in decorative style. They remind us of the strapwork on so many French cathedral doors, the Sainte-Anne door of Notre-Dame de Paris for example. The feet are formed simply by an extension of the wooden planks so that the chest may be raised off the damp floor. This fact already shows progress. Originally the chest was just a simple, rectangular parallelepiped; the addition of feet indicates an attempt to transform the essentially mobile and portable chest into a fixed piece of furniture that has its appointed place in the household. The lids of both chests are flat – they can therefore be used as seats. We can still see marks where a lock was fitted: they were evidently intended to hold precious objects.

2 | Furniture in General Use During the Fourteenth and Fifteenth Centuries

Towards the end of the Middle Ages, life gradually becomes more sedentary and the general atmosphere is favourable to the development of furniture. The variety of pieces is still very limited and although the chest remains the sole article of furniture used by most people, in some wealthy homes we find the first examples of chairs, benches, dressers, and, in rare cases, beds.

▶ *The Fourteenth-Century Chest*

The chest undergoes a transformation right at the beginning of the fourteenth century. Unfortunately hardly any authentic chests of this period are still extant, even in national collections. Repairs long since, or even recently, carried out on a great deal of furniture have altered it out of all recognition; whereas some pieces are incomplete, others are too complete and it is difficult for a furniture historian to draw definite conclusions. For instance, in the *Musée de Cluny* there exists a famous fourteenth-century chest called the *Pas Saladin* chest; its authenticity has been hotly disputed and only certain parts of it are genuinely old. However, this chest represents an interesting phase in the technical evolution of chests in general. It marks beyond any doubt a step forward from the strap-hinged chest. It is no longer cased in metal armour like a knight riding to a crusade, but richly carved in solid wood. The fourteenth-century *huchier* has ceased to be a simple carpenter, he already possesses many of those same tools which will continue to be used right up to the machine age; he is also able to employ stronger and more complex joints like the dovetail (see Chap. I, p. 21). This means that the iron strapwork can be discarded and the chest presents an

D

uninterrupted surface for decoration. The artisan also knows
how to choose his wood; instead of using rough-hewn timber,
which serves for general carpentry and furniture alike, the
fourteenth-century *huchier* now selects a special kind of wood.
In the *Pas Saladin* chest the large wooden planks are of stave-
wood (oak cut with the grain, used only for cooperage today),
containing no knots or sap layer. In spite of the fact that the
chest stands on attractively worked feet, it is still portable.
The elaborate decoration takes the form of tracery and is
sufficiently flat not to be damaged by knocks or blows. Yet
even so this chest still has grave faults; it is too heavy, and
although the wood is of exceptionally good quality, the planks
have become disjointed at the side and they break up the
decoration in an unsightly manner.

▶ *The Gothic Chest*

There were several solutions to the problem of visible joints.
A single massive plank could be used: this is what some
huchiers did in the fifteenth and sixteenth centuries, but it
meant hunting out very large, and therefore expensive, planks
and so this method could only be adopted for '*meubles de luxe*'.
Another solution was to alter the whole structure of the
furniture: this was when carved and panelled furniture
appeared. The Gothic chest nearly always consists of thick
uprights and traverses with mortise-and-tenon joints; narrow
wooden panels are tailed into these with tongue-and-groove
joints (see Chap. I, p. 21). There are many advantages to
this method: It means that the wood used can be cheaper
because the pieces are small and thinner; there is no difficulty in withstanding different degrees of heat and humidity
because the grooves allow the panels free play; also, a chest
constructed on this basis is lighter than the preceding types;
lastly, because the panels are sunk into the carcase, they are
further protected from knocks and blows and the carvings
can be executed in bolder relief. We should not forget, though,
that even in the fifteenth century, it was still essential for the
chest to be transportable.

Gothic chests are not hard to come by, but many of them
are wholly or partially fakes, since the 'cathedral' style that

was fashionable in about 1830 created a tremendous demand for this type of furniture. The decoration is nearly always the same. It is a close copy of ogival Gothic architecture, a reproduction in blind tracery of the Gothic cathedral fenestrations (see Plate II). Now that the *huchiers* have taken to working with a much more malleable material than stone, they let themselves go in elaborating on the decoration. The Flamboyant ogee arches have countless subdivisions filled with undulating curves and reverse curves, enclosing rosettes and quatrefoils and terminating in small bell-like motifs or often in heavily curved contours.

Another motif, employed mainly on the sides of chests or chairs, is the '*parchemin plyssé à drapperye*' or 'linenfold' motif. This motif does not derive from architecture at all; it might have had its origin in the skins that covered furniture in the previous age. When the hides were dry they contracted and overlapped in folds, and this may have given the *huchiers* the idea of reproducing a covering that had fallen into disuse.

'Parchment' folds may be represented as a simple fold of cloth or leather, but here again complication sets in and the folds are rendered in many different ways. This monotonous form of decoration was exploited to saturation point by fifteenth century *huchiers* on the commoner pieces of furniture or on parts which were least in evidence.

Another form of decoration appeared on chests: locks. They consisted of a metal box containing the bolt. This was generally a rectangular box attached to the chest by large, often clearly visible, nails and was attractively worked. The box was surrounded by an ironwork border cut out to look like lace; pinnacles or bell-like motifs were arranged on either side of the spaces left for the key and the hasp; shields were delicately engraved on the box. The hasp, which was hinged on to a piece of ironwork decoration, was itself also decorated: beetles, salamanders, chimeras, dragons with gaping jaws, and male or female busts, all figured on this piece of iron.

We have dwelt at length on the chest, not only because it was the commonest piece of medieval furniture, but because nearly all the other furniture of that era more or less directly derived from it.

▶ *The Throne Chair* (*chaire;* also called *chaière, chayère* and *cathèdre*, from the latin *cathedra*)

The throne chair is really no more than a chest with the rear uprights extended to form a high back, and the side uprights extended to form arm-rests. The throne chair definitely derived from the chest because the base is in itself a chest – frequently fitted with a lock. When it stood beside a bed, clothes were probably draped over it. It was decorated in the same way as the chest, but as it was nearly always draped with ornamental cloth hangings and cushions called *carreaux* which hid the seat base; the back was the only part to be decorated. Furthermore, this back decoration did not start below a point level with the head of a seated person; the lowest panel which acted as a back-rest was often left bare. In some cases the back extended upwards to form a canopy: the Anne de Bretagne chair in the *Musée des Arts Décoratifs* is an example. The lower part of this is a chest left unadorned, the upper part of the back is decorated with Flamboyant style arcading, and the canopy is draped with ermine.

The throne chair is a seat for state occasions. With the hangings draped over it, it is inconceivable that it could be placed anywhere but against a wall; in fact the reverse side of the chair-back is never decorated. The lord of the castle was the sole person to use it, either for presiding over meals or receiving homage from his vassals.

There are also some throne chairs for two people: for certain ceremonies the lord's wife would take her place beside her husband.

▶ *The Bench*

The chair was a fifteenth century creation but the bench existed long before that; it was also called a *form*, in French *forme* or *fourme* (from the vulgar latin *forma*). This, too, is none other than an adaptation of the chest; it now has arm-rests and a back. It is made in exactly the same way as the chair, but a bench of this type is very cumbersome and we know that at that same period there were some portable benches with no backs in existence, comprising one simple plank supported by two uprights. Its light weight is one of this seat's chief assets and the uprights are sometimes decorated with a delicate blind tracery. One of the benches in the *Musée des Arts Décoratifs* has this feature. Yet often this democratic, unpretentious seat was not decorated at all. It must have been treated with contempt in the following centuries as extremely few authentic benches are still in existence. There are also some smaller benches for one person, called benchlet (*banchel, bancel*) or stool (*escabeau, escabel*), which continued to be used in the next century.

▶ *The Buffet or Dressoir (Dresser)*

Both of these derive from the chest. They are, in fact, chests mounted on feet and opening at the front. The two names are usually interchangeable. It seems, however, that the *dressoir* was also identified with a *buffet de parade* and was used for displaying gold and silver plate for special ceremonies. Hardly any real *dressoirs* still exist and we are better acquainted with this article of furniture through the medium of inventories. It was made with shelves, their number strictly prescribed by etiquette; a prince had the right to four tiers but a baron only two.

The simple *buffet* assumes many different guises. The simplest example consists of a rectangular box, of which the two compartments called *guichets* are closed in by doors called *vantaux*. The doors are placed on either side of a central upright or a blind panel. It is in this piece of furniture that we find frieze drawers or *layettes* for the first time. Some *buffets* just have small rectangular panels below the large ones, but this space is also often occupied by frieze drawers. The base is left open; a single panel at the back is joined to the two (three or four) front uprights by arched or flattened stretchers bracketed together. The ornamentation is copied from the fifteenth-century chest and is strictly regulated by the division of the panels. These are decorated with the usual Flamboyant tracery fenestrations and linenfold carving on those parts not in evidence. Nevertheless we can see on this article of furniture (which was still rare in the fifteenth century) proof of a search for new types of decoration. Geometrical and floral motifs begin to replace the eternal fenestration. There is an example of this type of *buffet* in the *Musée des Arts Décoratifs*; on it we find *fleurs de lys* inscribed in lozenges decorating the façade doors. Generally, the uprights take the form of abutments or pinnacles, but they may be decorated with overlapping shell motifs. As with the chests, richly worked locks and bolts also contribute to the decoration.

▶ *Beds*

We might be justified in ending our short list of medieval furniture with the *buffet*, but a few beds certainly did exist. The two beds from the Château de Villeneuve in the *Musée des Arts Décoratifs* are proof of this. However archaic they may seem to us, these beds constitute a transition between the primitive, carpentry-made alcove bed – to which illustrated documents bear testimony, and of which there are many extant specimens east of the Rhine – and the sixteenth century alcove bed whose slender colonnettes replace the former solid sides. Only two sides of the beds mentioned here are panelled and a graceful, elegantly decorated colonnette at the fourth corner dispenses with the need to box in the bed completely. The decoration is still pure Gothic: linenfold panels on the bedstead and floral decoration on the frieze of the tester.

Of all the furniture we have studied so far, two pieces still occupy a place in our homes today: the coffer, or chest as it is now called, and the bench. True, these pieces do not provide present-day furniture manufacturers with any research material as regards decoration but the chest still has its place in hallways or children's playrooms. The bench is frequently used as a seat in country houses; it has even been introduced recently in towns where flats are cramped and we are glad of it because it can easily be slid under a table without taking up space.

Our medieval inheritance is meagre indeed as far as form is concerned; yet this is furniture strongly built and logically assembled whose decoration does no more than accentuate the grace and purity of line without breaking the rhythm, and it still holds a lesson for us. Furniture should be assembled in a straightforward manner with no technical 'acrobatics' to undermine its solidity; the decorative and architectural effect should not cause the structure to be weakened.

CHAPTER THREE

| RENAISSANCE

By the end of the fifteenth century life had become more sedentary, the middle-class had come into its own, ideas of comfort and well-being were the order of the day. People began to be tired of the eternal Flamboyant decoration – a wind of change and fresh invention was sweeping across the whole of Europe and through all spheres of life. It was over a century since Italian writers, architects, painters and sculptors had shaken off the yoke of their old Gothic tradition and launched out in search of new art forms. Although an artistic upheaval such as this did not go entirely unnoticed in France, it had little or no influence until French noblemen suddenly found themselves in direct contact with fifteenth-century Italy and its wonderfully prolific spirit of invention. Charles VIII, heedless of his father's shrewd politics, embarked on the phantom cause of reclaiming the Angevin possessions in Italy and, in the spring of 1495, descended as far as Naples. It was this military expedition that gave the French noblemen a sight of magnificent palaces full of gorgeous furniture and countless works of art. The craze took hold of them completely. It began with their barely concealed pillaging and continued after their return home with a study of the craftsmanship of their new possessions and an attempt to learn and imitate.

The Italian influence on French art was therefore twofold. Not only was the French aristocracy converted to a new conception of aesthetics, but contact with the great Italian families had taught the French that a nobleman owed it to himself to fill the role of promoter and protector of the arts. The king was not alone in this, for the noblemen, like Georges d'Amboise for instance, also made good use of Transalpine models; they became patrons of the arts and by their zealous enthusiasm inspired French, and even foreign, artists to create sumptuous residences for them. Thus a clientèle with new aesthetic requirements grew up. However, evolution in the decorative arts is slow. An artisan who has decorated his furniture with ogee motifs over a period of years cannot change his technique overnight, even though models are planted in front of him. Besides, whether he is conscious of it or not, he is bound by tradition. The new movement did not come into full force, at least as far as furniture was concerned, until the new generation of artists, born at the time of the Renaissance, had reached maturity; this was definitely much later, about mid-century. We may therefore distinguish two successive phases in the French Renaissance.

Under Charles VIII, Louis XII and François I (1494–1547) artists were content merely to transcribe new forms of decoration on to a medieval carcase. The Renaissance in furniture does not aspire beyond a very free interpretation of Lombard *quattrocento* motifs.

It was not until the reign of Henri II and his successors (1547–89) that the French creative genius really asserted itself. The artists of this period eagerly seized on new forms, studied them and adapted them. An architectural style was also emerging, in which a sense of balance and restraint counteracted its foreign origins. Some works already showed a pure classical spirit in their sense of correct proportions, their essentially French elegance and their distaste for excess.

1 | The Techniques

▶ *Joints and Types of Wood*

As always, the elegance of a piece of furniture is directly related to its technical perfection. The medieval *huchier* knew of no joints other than the mortise and tenon and the dove-

x *Arm-chair, Louis XV*

tail, but the sixteenth century *menuisier* discovered less obtrusive joints which could be hidden in the thickness of the
wood and thus leave the field clear for the carver to make a
continous decoration over the whole surface of the furniture.
Mitred and secret joints (see Chap. I, p. 21) released the
artist from having to abide by the rigorous divisions between
panels, as he had done in the previous age.

The range of woods increases. As carving becomes more and
more important, the *menuisier* tends to abandon oak in favour
of the softer walnut because it is easier to work; it also allows
a finer degree of carving and an interplay of light and shadow.
Ash – for veneers – cedar, ebony and lime – especially in the
South of France – make a tentative first appearance.

▶ *Decorative Processes*

Solid wood carving continues to be practised successfully all
through the Renaissance period, but new processes, particularly from mid-century onwards, were about to revolutionise
the appearance of French furniture. French artisans were
always somewhat reluctant to assimilate these new processes
borrowed from Italy, and in any case employed them very
sparingly. The article that most often gets the benefit of these
first attempts is the cabinet – also of foreign origin. There are
not many specimens in existence, because furniture decorated
in this way was exceedingly fragile and must have gone out
of fashion in a short time, but we are lucky in being
able to glean some accurate descriptions from inventories.
French artisans retained only three or four of the manifold
and ingenious methods used by the Italians to introduce
polychromy on furniture decoration; furthermore, these
methods were copied only in rare cases and on '*meubles de
luxe*'.

The process of *inlaying* a wood panel, previously carved out
to shape, with a motley assortment of pieces was called by the
Italians *tarsia* or *intarsia*. This *inlay-work* (see Chap. I, p. 26)
could be varied *ad infinitum* according to the design or materials
used.

In some cases the design is purely geometrical, but in
others it is intended to represent a picture (landscapes,

perspectives, genre scenes, even portraits); the Italians called this *intarsia pittorica.* This latter method was scarcely practised at all in France.

The materials inlaid were also very varied. Whilst the Italians had indulged their imagination and let it run riot, the French disciplined their striving for decorative effect: inlays were made of precious materials (gold, ivory) or minerals (variegated marble), natural wood (ebony) or perhaps even wood dyed by immersion in a bath of boiling oil; another method was to substitute the hard materials by a soft coloured paste. In France the artisans contented themselves with a faintly ivory-tinted paste kind of decoration called *moresque blanche.*

The Italians had reached such a degree of technical perfection that decoration had become a matter of supreme importance, overwhelming the structure. French artisans, on the other hand, seldom made this mistake and kept their coloured decoration discreetly under control. If an artist chose to use polychromy he simplified the shape of the piece and devoted only a small space to carving so that the new process would show up in its full glory.

Lastly, *marquetry* made its appearance at this point (see Chap. I, p. 31). This process stems from an entirely different technique, at which the Italians were past masters owing to their clever glue preparations. Here the decoration is actually stuck on to the carcase. Marquetry was the only one of all these processes to score a really resounding success in France. The word *marqueteur* was adopted into the French language in 1580 and official rules for the practice of marquetry were laid down in the guild statutes.

The general trend, therefore, is towards polychromy, and so French artisans manage to make a compromise. Furniture decoration still takes the form of traditional solid wood carving but, as a concession to contemporary taste which favours the introduction of colour, the projecting parts or those in high relief are gilt in silver or gold: shells, attributes of war, helmets, necklaces, crowns etc.

The latter process is still more interesting because, like marquetry, it has been perpetuated, though in a slightly different form. This sixteenth century innovation is the

origin of the magnificent bronze accessories with which
Boulle, Cressent and Gouthèire enriched their furniture.

2 | Decoration and Structure

Whilst Flamboyant decoration remained much the same for
two centuries of the Middle Ages, this was by no means the
case with the whole arsenal of motifs which French artisans
of the sixteenth century appropriated, and either copied or
adapted, from Italy. From Charles VIII to Henri IV progress
was slow and continuous. We still find hybrid furniture all
through Louis XII's reign: the plinth of a chair might for
example bear a linenfold decoration but its back would be
carved with grotesques. We have to wait until the reign of
François I before a pure Renaissance style in decoration is
evolved and the old themes eliminated; but with the accession
of Henri II, different motifs, different processes and different
structural forms again make a radical change in the appearance of furniture. The Renaissance set a wealth of new ideas
in train and this wonderfully prolific century saw a constant
renewal both as regards structure and decoration.

In consequence, any dividing line we choose to draw will
have to be an arbitrary one, though it is true that some motifs
were more popular in the first half of the century and others
in the second. For the purpose of this text, therefore, we will
stand by the traditional division into François I and Henri II
styles.

▶ *The François I Style*

The favourite motif here is that group of ornaments known as
grotesques. This is a word taken from the Italian, *grottesche*,
which describes a certain type of decoration used in ancient
times; it was rediscovered in Rome or the surrounding district
in places still hidden underground at the time (hence the
name grottoes). The 'Golden House' of Nero was a notable
example. This delicate and finely-chiselled form of decoration appears on the panels of wooden furniture just as often
as on the stone façades of the châteaux then being built.

Rigidly symmetrical planes are adorned with an untidy but harmonious conglomeration of divers realistic or fantastic fauna (griffons, dolphins, sphinxes, sirens, birds, etc.), realistic or stylised flora (here the acanthus leaf makes its début), and a tremendous variety of objects (vases, medallions Cornucopiae, trophies, etc.); human figures appear as masculine or feminine busts with or without arms; sometimes we also find the insertion of rectangular cartouches, called *écriteaux*, which bear some motto, emblem, coat of arms or heterogeneous collection of objects (daggers, plumes, bobbins, etc.). An element of order amongst all this bric-à-brac is supplied by the central motif: the stem of a flower, the shaft of a candelabrum or perhaps a bow of ribbon, from which these multifarious elements tumble forth in a rigid symmetry that alone makes such profusion feasible.

The second decorative element to make its début in this period is the pilaster. The pilaster is a convenient form of decoration for uprights. This, too, often carries grotesques; it is surmounted by various types of capital and according to the circumstances it broadens out or lengthens or is superposed *ad lib*. It also accentuates the way the furniture is divided into panels, exactly as in architecture, where it accentuates the different parts of a façade. Fluted or ringed columns were also known in the early Renaissance but the pilaster is generally most popular. Lastly, moulding takes a decisive step forward as the result of more advanced tools: the egg-and-darts, *raies de coeur* and pearl beading, which may still be found as late as Louis XVI, are here used for the first time.

The human figure also makes a tentative appearance at the beginning of the century. Like the ancients before them, the Italians dearly loved the beauty of human form. The early sixteenth century *huchier* appropriated it as a decorative motif, engraving it with the indelible stamp of his own personality; in this one item of the Renaissance repertoire we can see the different stages of development during the century reflected very clearly. At the start of the century the French artisan, who had lost none of the dash or verve of the old church carvers, remained loyal to the realist tradition of the Middle Ages: instead of slender figures in the refined Italian style, he carved crudely striking heads, busts and profiles which he inserted at intervals in his foliated scroll-work, interlaced floral designs or laurel wreaths. The human figure sometimes formed the central motif of a medallion or panel, but it bore evidence of keen, direct observation, and in some instances we might be tempted to label these images as portraits or even caricatures.

By the end of the century great progress had been made. We only need to compare the round embossed high reliefs of the François I period with the elegant, nude gods and goddesses carved in the low relief of the Jean Goujon style. Yet here again there were intermediate stages.

We could carry on almost indefinitely with the long list of fresh motifs that were introduced in this early Renaissance period. However, danger lay precisely in this wealth of variations. No wonder some artisans of poor taste got carried away with enthusiasm in the face of so many novelties and swamped their furniture with a confused and overwhelming mass of decoration! It needed a true artistic temperament and a keen sense of composition to preserve a unity of decoration – to create a work of art where balance and harmony would not be spoilt by lavish ornamentation.

▶ *The Henri II Style*

This first, somewhat uncontrolled creative outburst at the beginning of the century was soon checked by a new trend. The arrival in France in 1533 of the young Dauphine, Catherine de Médicis, who brought with her an elegant and resplendent court, contributed towards a fresh turn in the revival of French art. In addition to this, François I installed resident architects, painters, sculptors and even marquetry-workers, such as Jean Michael Pantaléon, at Court. This group of artists, which included as many Italians as Frenchmen, enjoyed the King's patronage and was commissioned by him to give new life and vigour to French art; it was known as the Fontainebleau school and its earliest achievements date back to approximately 1530. As far as furniture is concerned, the group's influence was not felt until about fifty years later, that is, some time after Henri II had come to the throne, hence the reason for calling it the 'Henri II style'.

The early Renaissance period affected only decoration of furniture; the second stage of the Renaissance saw the structure altered: this, therefore, is the period to which we are indebted for new furniture forms.

In François I's time, the typical artisan was given to imitating his discoveries in a haphazard fashion – he plundered the Transalpine repertoire of decorative motifs indiscriminately. Under Henri II, however, he proceeds quite differently. Architects, sculptors and designers (and individual artists were frequently accomplished in all these capacities) are well versed in their art and the elements they have borrowed; they now set about creating a new, essentially architectural style. A strictly mathematical approach supersedes the former unbridled imagination and the ancient classical orders are scrupulously observed. Although the artisan of this era proves himself more competent technically, he is less of an artist than his predecessor because he just copies models as they are presented to him in pattern-books of ornamental furnishings. What the artisan gains in dexterity he loses in spontaneity and sincerity. Hence the reason why furniture of this period is often forbidding, severe and rather formal, for the profuse, intricate decoration is too deliberately contrived and the structure is too hidebound by the stringent rules of classical art. Although Henri II furniture quickly assumes classic qualities of tranquillity and balanced harmony, its composition is too academically calculated and pedantic.

These new principles are reflected most clearly in the *buffet* (see Plate II). It becomes a small-scale version of an architectural façade; we find architectural elements even in the detail of carved decoration (triglyphs, guttae, cornices, friezes, pediments). The *buffet* stands on a plinth supported by square, knob, bun or claw feet, or better still, couchant animals: in the latter case they have clearly been taken direct from Italy. The lower section may have one or more doors, but the real novelty lies in the manner in which the artist treats the uprights. His inspiration stems directly from current architectural practice. We find a choice of broad pilasters, round or flat balusters, engaged or free-standing columns, single or in pairs, or caryatids (see Glossary).

These might be figures of women or classical monsters such as sphinxes, griffons, tritons, etc. The lower section is kept distinct from the upper section by a cornice, by gadrooning (frequently found during the next period and a favourite theme in Flemish decoration), or by the addition of one or two frieze drawers placed above or below the cornice according to the circumstances.

The upper section is nearly always treated independently and has lighter proportions; it is quite common for a base comprising two doors to be furnished with a single door on the upper section. Even if the *buffet* has two doors above and two below, the top ones are more often than not narrower and shallower. Athough it is almost a standard rule for the two units to be different sizes, this lack of uniformity can be redressed by adding volutes or chimeras on to the sides. Pilasters, balusters and columns frame the upper as well as the lower section and support a traverse with some form of pediment on top. We seldom come across a piece of Renaissance furniture that does not boast triangular or curved pediments, usually broken to make room for a niche that harbours a statuette; and, as a crowning piece of clumsiness, this niche is itself surmounted by a small pediment. However, most of these fragile pediments have disappeared and the only evidence of their existence are the marks left where they were fixed on.

Another version of the *buffet*, closer to that made in the Middle Ages but likewise copied from building façades, consists of an upper section constructed over an open gallery. The uprights (columns, balusters or pilasters) are either free-standing or linked by low, arched stretchers. These structural elements are really purely conventional; in the first type of *buffet* the colonnettes have nothing to do with supporting the carcase and the structure would not suffer if they were removed; the columns, which serve no practical purpose at all, are never without stylobates or capitals – Ionic, Doric or Tuscan. The broken pediment, which is almost a ritual, makes an already cumbersome *ensemble* even more heavy – and quite needlessly so. The rigid division between sections is accentuated by a more complicated form of moulding (see Chap. I, p. 24) than in the previous period, enriched with ornamental motifs copied very closely from classical antiquity: gadrooning, fluting, interlaced patterns, rosettes, palmettes. The uprights – balusters or pilasters – are also carved with grotesques but more often with plumes or acanthus leaves in flowing, simple lines, or, yet again, with lozenges enclosing various emblems or attributes. The panels are still decorated with medallions but they may be supported by mythological gods and goddesses in academic poses, or surrounded by types of scrolls called *cuirs découpés*. Pure geometrical motifs and cunning architectural perspectives also remain in fashion until the end of the century.

Everything, therefore, is sacrificed to decorative effect: joints are no longer in evidence, neither are any pains spared in concealing every detail which might possibly remind the onlooker that furniture was anything else but a piece of architecture; pintles, hinges, handles, whether drop or otherwise, are also made as unobtrusive as possible.

Yet French genius rebelled against the over-strict application of these rules and the craftsmen's individual temperaments counteracted such an impersonal and oppressively solemn approach.

Having passed through a phase of uniform Gothic rule, furniture now emerges in a multitude of different local styles. True, the royal household does set a fashion, but its sway is limited because the great noblemen have not yet come to live at Court; they live in the provinces where they patronise local artists. In 1885 Bonnaffé attempted to map out a 'geography' of Renaissance furniture; furniture historians have each tried to add one more stone to this edifice ever since, but we have to admit that any assertion in this respect will always be guesswork. We do not have a sufficient number of pieces, let alone authentic pieces for which we know the exact date and place of manufacture, to enable us to draw any definite conclusions. However tempted we may be to divide furniture of this period into regional schools, we cannot base our assumptions on anything more than rough generalisations. What we can do, though, is to pick out some styles associated with certain outstanding artistic personalities: Jean Goujon, Jacques Androuet du Cerceau, and Hugues Sambin (see Plate III); other styles such as the Auvergnat, Lyonnais, or

XI *Buffet, Louis XV*

Provençal are the result of unique local conditions; nevertheless all attempts at classification must remain very much open to debate.

3 | The Different Types of Furniture

A curious little work by one Gilles Corrozet, entitled *Les Blasons Domestiques*, published at Lyon in 1537, will give anyone who wishes to study the different kinds of sixteenth-century furniture a thread to follow through the labyrinth. The excellent Gilles Corrozet's verses are doubtless a trifle superficial and give us only a vague idea of decoration and structure, but they do at least tell us whether this or that piece of furniture was in current use. We may also note that, contrary to what we might have imagined, the chest still holds a place of honour among the mass of sixteenth-century furniture.

▶ *The Chest*

Naturally, the prodigious use of chests in the fifteenth century does not cease overnight. Extremely beautiful chests are made all through the sixteenth century, since this article of furniture still has some function; we no longer expect it to be portable, but we do still expect it to provide a safe place for keeping clothes until a more appropriate piece of furniture will arrive on the scene. In order to make access to it easier, and to display the richly decorative carving to better advantage, it gradually became the custom to raise it on a plinth. This support is in fact a low table with very short feet often taking the form of lions' paws.

The structure of the chest alters. Whereas in Gothic times the strict division into equal panels is observed, in the Renaissance free rein is given to every whim of the imagination. The façade is sometimes formed by one wide panel flanked by two narrow panels, sometimes one narrow panel flanked by two wide panels, or sometimes large and small panels alternated. From François I onwards we frequently find chest façades composed of a single panel. Panel sizes are

XII *Coiffeuse, Louis XV*

E

therefore extremely varied and it is no longer a question of the decoration being adapted to a predetermined arrangement of panels, but of the panels being adapted to the decoration chosen to adorn them. There is an almost inviolable law of the Renaissance that the uprights should not be left bare, as they had been in the preceding age: they are ornamented with pilasters, balusters, columns and chimeras which frame the panels and accentuate the corners of the chest. The carved motifs echo the new fashion: mythological scenes (Neptune recumbent in a cartouche of scrolls and fruit), biblical scenes (the 'Baptism of Christ', 'Herod', 'Herodias' and 'St. John') or allegories (death holding an arrow and shovel and preparing to fight the nobility and the clergy). Medallions or mirrors (plain, convex medallions) surrounded by volutes or upheld by cherubs are also used for decoration.

▶ *The Buffet or Dresser* (see Plate IV)

In the early sixteenth century this piece of furniture was no different, at least as far as structure was concerned, from the medieval *buffet*, but as we have already seen, radical changes were to come about during the course of the century. *Buffet* is therefore the name given to an article of furniture consisting of cupboard compartments and small drawers, supported either by pillars or, shortly afterwards, by a solid base also containing cupboard compartments. It was a mistake that this article ever came to be called a *crédence* because this is generalising a specific and short-lived title. As it happened, an Italian fashion was prevalent at Court under Henri III. The idea then occurred to 'go one better' and honour the traditional *buffet* with a name taken from the Italian word *credenzia*; a *credenzia* in Italy meant a particular piece of furniture on which meat and drink was placed and tested before being served to the master of the house. This custom, which was fully justified in Renaissance Italy when poisoning was rife, did not extend beyond the Court in France and gave rise to no fresh inventions in furniture; the *buffet* served such a purpose. When studies of early sixteenth-century *buffets* were made, the word '*crédence*' was apt to be used because it sounded better than *buffet*. However, this term should be eliminated as it is not to be found either in Corrozet, or in the inventories of that period, or in listed collections of ornaments.

There is an infinite number of versions of the *buffet*, both in structure and in decoration, but its function is not at all clearly defined. Unlike the previous period, it was in daily use, but could be placed in the bedroom, the kitchen or the main hall. It served to display plate, but also housed linen, clothes and precious objects.

Ought we to speak of cupboards in the sixteenth century? Corrozet makes no mention of them and at this stage any distinction between cupboards and *buffets* is purely arbitrary. It is true that by the end of the century there were *buffets* with one door, very different from those made at the beginning of the century which were always double-bodied and had several doors, but the cupboard properly speaking did not come into being until the next century.

▶ *The Cabinet*

The cabinet is a very difficult piece of furniture to define. It was imported or copied from foreign models and appears in a great variety of shapes and sizes. At first it seems to be simply a small coffer with two handles attached, containing a number of drawers concealed by one or more doors, or a drop-front which serves as a small writing-table. A cabinet of this kind stands on a table, coffer or trestle supports. Gradually it is fixed on to a specially made support and gets to be almost identical with the *buffet*. By the end of the century it occasionally takes on a monumental design and bears a façade of crowded columns with bases and capitals. In any event it is a high-class article of furniture.

▶ *The Table*

The reader will remember that a fixed table was unheard of in the Middle Ages. The sixteenth-century artisan on the other hand invents complicated, many-sided tables and is guided in his imitation of Italian styles solely by the designs of the *ornemanistes*.

In its simplest form, the Renaissance table is composed of a massive top whose frieze is decorated with gadroons, inter-laced and egg-and-dart mouldings, flutes, acanthus leaves, etc. This top rests on four legs, joined in pairs by rail-bases; these rails are in turn linked together by a cross-stretcher. As Renaissance tables are distinctly higher than our modern ones (32 inches to 36 inches), the traverse would have pro-vided a foot-rest. This relatively simple form soon becomes complicated, since the artisan's attention to rich carving increases with his technical skill. Columns or, better still, a series of arcades occupy the space between the table-top and the cross-stretcher. Legs turn into balusters, pilasters and caryatids. The rail-bases are embellished with carvings (sea-horses or animals couchant); alternatively they are pierced (perforated leaves or mascarons), in order to lighten the overall effect.

Du Cerceau provided many examples of another style wherein the table-top is placed on two uprights in the shape of a wide-open fan (see Plate v). This innovation was a copy of the ancient classic *cartibulum* and it inspired the *maîtres ornemanistes* and the artisans to indulge in a regular orgy of fantasy. We find a mixed assortment of griffons, addorsed satyrs, terms or female half-figures tapering into pedestals and confronted animals (rams, eagles with outspread wings, chimeras with lions' paws). There are some gorgeous speci-mens of these highly original tables, attributed to Hugues Sambin, in the Besançon and Dijon museums.

Draw-top tables, so popular for modern furnishings, make their début in France during this period. They were called double tables because, when they are folded up, the upper half of the table-top conceals a lower half which is divided at the centre into two equal parts.

▶ *Seat Furniture*

When a radical change occurs in social life it always has a direct influence on seat furniture, since it is directly concerned with the question of social precedence. In the Middle Ages there were two state chairs: the faldstool and the throne chair. The metal faldstool as a ceremonial chair disappeared at the beginning of the sixteenth century, but its shape was perpetuated: evidence of this may be found in inventories which record 'hinged folding chairs', 'pincer chairs', 'folding chairs', 'folding stools', etc., which are simply faldstools made in wood.

The *throne chair* is still reserved for high-ranking persons. It keeps its monumental aspect for a long time, for although decoration may have changed in the early years of the century, structural forms were slow to evolve. Originally it was a derivation of the chest, but later on the arm-rests cease to be made of solid panels; they consist in a moulded traverse fitted on to a pierced framework. A decidedly more manageable version of the throne chair, called an arm-chair, also appears at this juncture (see Plate VIII). This is a seat resting on four columns joined together at the base by solid traverses. The back is pierced. In addition to the bench or stool (*bancelle, escabelle, placet, selle, tabouret,* etc.) that continue from the Middle Ages, we find ladies' chairs (*chaises de femmes*) – low, with a high back – and the *caquetoire,* a trapezoid seat resting either on four legs or on a single pivot.

▶ Beds

Renaissance beds are extremely rare. They are no different from those at the end of the fifteenth century. They usually take the form of a box frame with four uprights placed at the corners. The originality of the bed depends to a great extent on the manner in which the uprights are treated. At the beginning of the century these are usually slender colonnettes grouped together or fluted; but under Henri II the job of supporting the tester is more often taken over by strapping telamones or cumbersome caryatids. Pedestal terms are also used, some of which may have been inspired by Hugues Sambin, or pilasters, many examples being supplied by du Cerceau. The bed-head is the most important feature; it is always magnificently decorated.

Thus, step by step, we have followed up the innovations made in the art of furniture during the Renaissance. The progress achieved is tremendous. The late sixteenth century *menuisier* now has a practically inexhaustible fund of decorative motifs at his disposal. In the centuries that follow, he merely draws on his reserves, choosing whatever corresponds best to the taste of the period. As far as form is concerned, there are not many innovations. The one and only type of medieval *buffet* with fixed proportions has been supplanted by the Renaissance *buffet* with many combinations of proportions, and the cabinet. The one and only type of throne chair has been succeeded by the arm-chair, lady's chair and *caquetoire*. Lastly, the sixteenth century sees a variety of tables almost as great as in the eighteenth century.

The rising sap of fresh invention at the beginning of the century had almost dried up by the end of Henri II's reign and such an amazing quantity of material needed to be pruned. Yet this role was not to be undertaken by the period immediately following when *menuisiers* were content to make what were often indiscriminate copies of Renaissance models. Fifty years were to pass before the highly original and multifarious innovations of the sixteenth century were disciplined, sorted out and co-ordinated.

CHAPTER FOUR

| LOUIS XIII

It is customary to give the title of 'Louis XIII' to a transition
period which, in fact, starts from the death of Henri III
(1589) and continues right through to Louis XIV's seizure of
personal power (1661). The Renaissance died out long before
the end of the sixteenth century. As soon as the troubles over
religious wars began, original creative work became more and
more of a rarity; the country had reached such a low ebb
that even Henri IV's accession and the Edict of Nantes failed
to re-establish a congenial atmosphere for art to flourish in.
In 1608 Henri IV did well to take the initiative and install
privileged artisans in the Louvre galleries, but these artisans
were either foreigners or French artists whom the King had
sent to Flanders for their artistic training. Although this
course of action partly solves the economic problem – scarcely
any more foreign furniture is imported now that it is made on
the spot in France – the artistic problem remains as great as
ever: artisans such as these cannot hope to create a national
art. Two years later the kingdom fell into the hands of a
queen-regent; and two foreign queens, who exerted an
excessively profound influence thanks to two long minorities,
succeeded one another on the throne of France. Marie de
Médicis was Florentine but also a devotee of Flemish art,
Anne of Austria was Spanish but she was dominated by an
Italian cardinal. What could Louis XIII possibly do in his
brief, personal reign to halt or combat these prevailing
influences?

Hence the reason why French art has to struggle to assert itself for more than half a century while being subjected to highly cosmopolitan influences. A series of attempts, sometimes failures and sometimes successes, stand out as landmarks in a period of confusion like this where there are no clearly distinguishable characteristics.

A kind of scission takes place in furniture; on the one hand we have the middle classes and minor nobility who, having acquired a taste for furnishing their homes during the Renaissance, continue to use sixteenth-century furniture with very few alterations; on the other we have the Court which is almost entirely foreign and either sends to Italy, Spain or the Netherlands for its furniture, or orders French artisans to reproduce foreign models as faithfully as possible.

▶ *Middle-Class Furniture*

The Henri II style, so original when it first came into fashion, has difficulty in acquiring fresh vitality. Naturally, we cannot expect forms based on erudite and ingenious imitations of a foreign art to retain their vigour for long. Less than fifty years after the height of the Renaissance, under the last of the Valois Kings and Henri IV, the typical artisan finds himself sentenced to making endless reproductions; he carries out the set formulae without any personal feeling behind them. The same mistakes crop up three centuries later, under the Second Empire, when the Henri II style is copied again.

What modifications did the Louis XIII period bring to this traditional furniture?

Decoration and form both grow imperceptibly coarser and heavier. All the Renaissance motifs still take pride of place, though it may be worth noticing, in passing, that plumes and crossed palms occur a little more often. Perhaps the greatest change that comes in with the early seventeenth century is a new approach to floral decoration. The stylised flowers and restrained scrollwork typical of the Renaissance are supplanted in the Louis XIII period by fat bouquets of natural, 'living' flowers, heavy-hanging garlands, clusters of fruit and thick foliage that spill out in great sheaves from

XIII *Console d'Applique, Louis XV*

bulging cornucopiae. Cartouches and mascarons are also infected by this fever of opulence: they grow bigger; their edges become thick and swollen; the volutes follow a slow, majestic curve. Thus everything combines to give an impression of a life of plenty and of purely materialistic riches.

The structure of furniture alters little. No really new methods are adopted. The artisans are satisfied with generalisations, variations and modifications of techniques previously used under the Renaissance.

In the Louis XIII period *lathe-turning* is the chief process adopted in decorating uprights and traverses: table-legs and stretchers, chair uprights and traverses, colonnettes at the corners of *buffets* and cabinets – everything is turned. With imagination and skill a *menuisier* can obtain many variations in turning methods. In fact turning may take the form of pearl beading (small, round beads in a continuous line), spirals (either a simple spiral or one with a fillet at the bottom of the groove), balusters, pears, vases, peg-top feet, etc. The uprights are usually turned from left to right, but on pieces of fine craftsmanship two uprights facing each other are sometimes turned in opposite directions. Different kinds of turning may be also used to decorate one and the same piece: for example, a spirally turned traverse may be broken in the centre by a circular turned motif. When a square-section member is turned, the square shape is retained at points where the member needs maximum strength; for example, chair-legs keep their square section at points where they are jointed to the cross-stretchers and to the cornice at the top. On the other hand we may equally come across purely decorative colonnettes applied to the corners of *buffets*, these colonnettes being sawn in half lengthwise and glued on to the real, functional uprights.

Apart from turning, one of the commonest processes employed during the Louis XIII period is *moulding*. Here again we see few original ideas in the early seventeenth century. The different sections of a piece of furniture are accentuated by a more generous, thicker and more highly developed moulding than the Renaissance kind; but whereas under the Renaissance moulding has no greater purpose than to show up the delicate carving on the panels, in the Louis XIII period, heavy, complicated mouldings frequently take over the entire decoration of some pieces: such broad, cumbersome mouldings make an emphatic frame for cornices, panels, plinths, drawer-fronts, etc. (see Plate VI).

Moulding even thrusts its way into the centre of panels, ousting the carved motifs of the preceding period. We find panels cut in a great variety of geometrical combinations: lozenges enclosing squares, lozenges subdivided into triangles, etc. If, in framing his triangles with mouldings, the artisan chooses to make them stand out in relief, he then obtains a surface studded with little pyramids. This is called diamond-point decoration (see Plate VI). If, by way of an alternative, the artisan chooses to carve a circular, concentric moulding, this kind of relief is called *gâteau*. There are an infinite number of different moulding profiles, hence a series of particularly graphic names (*tas de sable* for example) which are nevertheless subject to controversy. There is not much, therefore, that is new in the general run of furniture; innovations are reserved for exceptional pieces ordered by the Court.

▶ *Court Furniture*

Traditional furniture was made of oak, walnut or pearwood, but, as a result of foreign influences, the Court developed a craze in the early seventeenth century for exotic and precious woods. Ebony in particular, which had already been known and used during the Renaissance for fillets or small pieces of decoration, was outrageously popular; it was so much in demand that imitations were made with pearwood dyed black on cheap pieces, or on the least visible parts of the '*meubles de luxe*'. The corporation Statutes of 1645 prohibited this practice. However, it would have been too costly, not to say impossible, to import enough ebony to manufacture whole articles of furniture. The *ébéniste* – the term '*menuisier en ébène*' appears in the Corporation Statutes in 1608 – represents a new technique (see Glossary). He saws the valuable ebony into sheets just thick enough (about 8 mm.) to be carved in a low relief. He then glues the plaques thus obtained on to a carcase of cheap wood – sometimes even common deal. This technique, which is an intermediate stage between working in solid wood and veneering, opens up the way to new decorative processes; the artist is now able to carve, in very low relief, mythological, battle or religious scenes, often reflecting a Flemish exuberance and intricacy, or he may engrave foliated scrolls, flowers and geometrical patterns. The finished effect is magnificently rich: the interplay of light and shadow over the ebony's many gleaming facets, and the clear-cut, sharp-angled carvings, present a singular combination of splendour and beauty.

Inlaid furniture is no less common. The technique is not new but the range of materials never ceases to expand: we find a wide assortment of stones (jasper, cornelian, lapis-lazuli, agate), exotic woods (kingwood, purplewood, cedar and ebony of course), metals (pewter, brass, gold and silver) and animal products (tortoise-shell, ivory, mother-of-pearl, bone, even pearls).

Mosiac work is all the rage for a short time: Marie de Médicis brought this process, highly prized in Tuscany, into fashion. It entails taking rare stones cut in cubes and fitting them together in patterns; it was mainly used on flat-topped pieces of furniture.

Marquetry is still practised too. Coloured woods begin to appear alongside pewter, ivory and silver. For instance we find highly elaborate, naturalistic floral motifs in wood mosaic set against a background of ebony.

These processes, whether executed separately or in combination, all add to the overcharged appearance of furniture, and we cannot help but hesitate when faced with these inordinately rich pieces; is this really French furniture? Even in cases where we are able to ascertain that it was definitely made in France – and such cases are extremely rare – we are aware that it represents a break with national tradition. In the early seventeenth century there was a vogue for all things European. There was only one way in which a courtier, be he French, Italian or Spanish, could manage to keep his furnished apartments up to date in style, and that was to collect his furniture from as many different countries as he could. His table might be English, his cabinet Italian, his chairs Spanish, yet they would all go together to make a harmonious *ensemble* because both the artists and the processes they used were common to the whole of Western Europe.

Foreign techniques and structural forms both have a repercussion on the art of French furniture-making. Some of the forms are preserved; after being modified and adapted they become such an integral part of French technique that we forget their origin: tortoise-shell and brass marquetry (perfected by J.-C. Boulle in the seventeenty century and continued into the eighteenth and nineteenth centuries) becomes a French speciality; coloured wood marquetry, in the hands of the eighteenth-century *ébénistes*, gives rise to such exquisite masterpieces that it is in itself the hallmark of French furniture in its most glorious phase.

1 | The Different Types of Furniture

We can call on various sources of information for furniture belonging to the middle classes and nobility. Whereas in the previous period we had a versifier, Gilles Corrozet, for our guide, we turn this time to an engraver, Abraham Bosse, to instruct us on his contemporary furniture. Bosse was familiar only with interiors of the well-to-do classes, but when we examine his engravings in detail we are able to draw conclusions which would not have crossed our minds at all if our studies had been confined to museum pieces alone.

For instance, we never find a high-backed arm-chair in Bosse's engravings. We may therefore suppose that the high-backed arm-chair is still considered to be a state chair, in the way that the 'throne chair' had been in previous periods; the middle classes were content with a low-backed arm-chair. As far as we can see from Bosse, cupboards appear to be in current use, yet they do not occur very often in inventories and as museum pieces they are exceptional. The turned wooden seats, apparently so characteristic of the Louis XIII period, were not perhaps so common as we might be tempted

to suppose. In Bosse's engravings the seats are more often
made as a crudely assembled wooden framework, completely
covered (including the legs) with material, held in place by
nails. They were thus easily transportable at a time when the
owners were still inclined to move house often, but evidently
both material and carcase have disappeared. It would therefore appear that turning was a process reserved exclusively for
pieces of considerable luxury.

We must be careful not to draw too hard and fast conclusions from these last observations. Firstly, Bosse's observations
were clearly confined to a very narrow category of interiors
and secondly, both national and private collections tend
generally to keep the rare and luxury specimens rather
than the common ones. However, it does furnish us with
a useful premise to compare these two sources of information.

As for the sumptuous furniture at Court where money was
no object, this is minutely and helpfully described in various
famous inventories (Mazarin, 1653; Anne of Austria, 1666,
etc.). These are our most reliable sources concerning the
very un-French furnishing of aristocratic interiors.

▶ *Buffets, Cupboards and Cabinets*

The traditional double-bodied *buffet* with four doors, standing
on a plinth and crowned by a heavy pediment, remains in
normal everyday use. In order to keep in line with contemporary taste, the plinth is made to rest on lions' paws or
flattened bun feet (see Plate vi); it may also be carved with
some extraneous decorative motifs, or its panels may sometimes be gouged out in a robust diamond-point design; the
pilasters or balusters that used to serve as uprights are
replaced by turned members.

Single-bodied *buffets* with one or two doors only are already
being made – these are no more than cupboards. We can
also classify relatively low furniture with four doors, copied
more or less directly from the Netherlands, under the heading of cupboards.

The cabinet still stays as a luxury piece only and is tremendously popular. It is imported from Italy, Germany, the

Netherlands, Spain. Cardinal Mazarin has no less than twenty in his possession, each one more grossly over-elaborate than the next. At the close of the century the cabinet begins to depreciate badly and often gets destroyed – which explains its rarity today. Those cabinets still surviving are generally of much simpler type. Most of them are cased in ebony, square and massive, since the nature of ebony precludes curved surfaces. The sole decoration on these austere pieces is the delicate, flattened relief carving on the panels and the gleaming polished surface of the ebony itself.

▶ *Tables and Bureaux*

Tables resting on fan-shaped supports at either end disappear. All that remain are small-sized tables standing on turned legs, heavily intertwined. Stretchers are of H- or X-form. The centre-point is indicated by a different kind of turning from the rest of the traverse – a vase, knob, peg-top or some other ornament may be added. The cornice is often gadrooned and the flat top surrounded by an ovolo moulding.

The bureau makes its appearance. According to whether he is concerned with reading or writing as an occupation, the gentleman of the period alternates between two standard types: the *bureau pupitre* (writing-desk), or the table. Writing tables occur in sixteenth-century inventories. Henri IV appears to have been the first person to want a bureau combining a table-top for writing with a series of drawers or pigeon-holes in which his documents could be locked up and filed away. This design was repeated several years later for the Maréchal de Créqui's bureau (prior to 1638). Most people, of course, had to be satisfied, as they were in the sixteenth century, with a table covered with drugget cloth or some quite different, lighter material, but the forerunner of the cylinder top desk (*bureau à cylindre*) was born in the early seventeenth century.

▶ *Seat Furniture*

In about 1636 – it is difficult to specify the exact date because the two names are valid at the same time – chairs with arms are given the definitive title of *fauteuils* (arm-chairs). From now onwards arm-chairs always feature arm-rests and a broad back. Louis XIII arm-chairs have hard, straight backs. State arm-chairs have high backs, but in most cases backs are low. Sometimes they are square but they can also be broader than they are high. Legs are generally turned. They are invariably linked by cross-stretchers and the front legs are joined higher up by an extra traverse, richly carved and occasionally decorated with a coat of arms. The consoles supporting the arm-rests are formed by an upward extension of the legs. Arm-rests are straight and terminate in lions' heads, rams' heads or female busts.

The word *chaise* (chair) begins to be used when specifically referring to seats without arm-rests. The chair has the same characteristics as the arm-chair described above; towards mid-century, the lady's chair (*chaise de femme*) which dates back to the François I period, begins to be called a *chaise à vertugadin.* The fashion for hoop skirts, or farthingales as they were called, meant that skirts were voluminous and prevented women from sitting comfortably in arm-chairs. The back is usually decorated with some foliated motif; the seat, which is often trapezoid, rests on four turned legs slanting outwards to the ground. The vogue for *chaises a vertugadin* lasted just as long as the farthingales themselves and disappeared at the beginning of Louis XIV's reign.

The great innovation of this period comes when the *carreaux* are discarded and replaced by fixed upholstery, nailed straight on to the framework. A layer of horse-hair covered by some coarse material or sheepskin acts as a foundation for this upholstery which might take the form of cowhide or embossed leather, either gilt or painted *à la mauresque.* There are also some chairs in existence covered in needlework tapestry, in *gros* or *petit point,* or more simply still, in fabric (velvet, satin, brocade, taffeta, etc.). The large-headed nails by which the upholstery is fixed on to the wooden seat also provide an element of decoration: with their large, rounded shape and careful spacing they can be made into all sorts of pattern combinations.

We should make a special mention here of cane chairs,

which appeared at this stage; they were richly decorated and the fact that Abraham Bosse does not depict them in his engravings leads us to assume that they were still considered to be luxury seats at the time. For their origin we have to look to Holland where the East India Company regularly imported cane from the Far East; these pieces of cane were cut in thin strips and threaded through little holes pierced in the framework. There are some very fine specimens of these chairs in French museums but it is difficult to find out whether we are confronted with furniture that was really made in France. However, no matter whether cane chairs started off by being French or not, they ended up by taking their place among the range of chairs used in the following periods.

We cannot talk of Louis XIII beds because beds were the monopoly of the *Tapissier*'s art. We have not inherited any wooden parts of a bed that were intended to be seen and might have been saved from destruction. We should merely put it on record that for roughly a century, from 1570 to approximately 1670, materials and draperies have a major role to play in the history of furniture. Not only beds, but tables and chairs too, are submerged under fabric coverings.

This period, which has often been unjustly dismissed because it is wedged between two culminating points in the evolution of French art, did not slip by, however, without leaving some mark on the history of furniture. Although the decorative processes, with their over-abundant carvings, their gaudy, multi-coloured mosaics and marquetry designs, do not appeal to our present-day taste, we must admit that these florid exaggerations did give birth to some interesting techniques such as the use of exotic woods for veneering brass and tortoise-shell marquetry, etc. Innovations in form had an even more far-reaching effect: the modified version of the *buffet* engendered the *armoire* (cupboard) which was to have a long career in years to come; the first of the *bureaux* were made and from henceforward they are an integral part of all standard *ensembles*; finally, we have an interesting and definitive premise by which we may clarify the outstanding

XIV *Small Table, Louis XV*

question of chairs: from now on chairs and arm-chairs have very distinct characteristics.

The task of sifting and co-ordinating these extremely varied experiments falls to the next period, yet it is impossible for such an attempt at rationalisation to come about without decoration and form being first considerably impoverished.

xv *Bergère, Louis XV*

F

CHAPTER FIVE

LOUIS XIV |

It was not until about 1660 that a genuinely French style began to be established. For two centuries past France had drawn on foreign resources to replenish her stock of decorative motifs, but in mid-seventeenth century the tide of artistic development turns. France now becomes the country where innovations are made, the well to which all other countries come to draw inspiration for several centuries hence. Yet France does not rest on her own laurels; she remains open to all influences, but her creative powers and capacity for assimilation are so strong that she is instantly able to make all those elements which she borrows from other countries her own, even from such far distant ones as China and Japan. The king plays a leading part in the evolution of classical art. After the Renaissance, artists were obliged to pander to the whims and caprices of taste displayed by the king and his Court – their chief customers – but there was no overall policy imposed to guide or co-ordinate individual effort. From 1661 onwards the situation was totally different. France's new Sovereign was imbued with visions of grandeur and glory; he wanted a sumptuous, impressive setting created around himself and his Court, one that would raise French royal prestige in the eyes of the whole world. The king was therefore the master craftsman who engineered France's artistic supremacy in the second half of the seventeenth century, and never was a title better justified than that of the 'Louis XIV style'.

However, the king's wishes alone would not have been enough to realise those perfectly coherent *ensembles* had they been created by artists working independently. We owe the practical solution of the problem to Colbert. Ever since 1662, as Superintendent of Royal Palaces, he had been negotiating to buy the manufactory and surrounding lands on the banks of the Bièvre belonging to the Gobelins brothers, dyers in scarlet. He had ordered the erection of buildings and gathered a group of artists together. In 1667 everything was ready for the king to proclaim an edict and institute *'la Manufacture Royale des Meubles de la Couronne'*. Lebrun was put in charge of this vast enterprise in which the official (classical) art flourished for nearly thirty years. An artist like Lebrun was an extremely judicious choice, since he had taken up residence in 1658 at Vaux-le-Vicomte in Fouquet's employ, and had there taken it on himself to study every branch of the decorative arts. The role of First Painter to the King was two-fold: on one hand he administered the manufactory and co-ordinated the work of the different *ateliers*, on the other, he supplied all kinds of models for the sculptors, engravers, goldsmiths, weavers and *'menuisiers en ébène et en bois'* (i.e. cabinet-makers) who were under contract to furnish the royal palaces. Conditions for artistic activities were never more favourable. The demand was colossal; not only did the Louvre and Versailles have to be furnished but there were the Trianon, Fontainebleau, Saint-Germain and Marly. The king never counted the cost; this was the time when his artisans had no hesitation in making furniture out of solid silver.

It was at this moment too that consideration was given for the first time to interior decoration as an *ensemble*. The architects and *maîtres ornemanistes* play an ultra-important part in the scheme. They supply designs not only for windows and doors but ceilings, fireplaces, bas-reliefs, candelabra, girandoles, tapestries, furniture, etc. Lebrun's fertile imagination and immense activity, coupled with his rise to fame, made him the principal founder of Louis XIV art. Yet besides him there were veritable dynasties of artists like the Lepautres: Jean (1618–82) and Antoine (1621–91); the Marots: Jean (1619–79), Daniel (1650–1712), and Pierre (d. 1716); and the

Bérains: Jean (1630–1711), Claude (d. 1726?), and Jean II (1674–1726), all of whom devoted themselves unceasingly to engraving a collection of designs which artisans were obliged to refer to if they wished their work to be acceptable in the general scheme of decoration.

The *menuisier* and the *ébéniste*, therefore, are no longer the original creators; they take their inspiration directly from the work of the *maîtres ornemanistes* but they modify the usually very complicated designs put before them, because it would have been impossible to translate them exactly in terms of wood. In this way furniture is closely governed by the general principles of order and majesty that dominate art from 1660 onwards. Little by little furniture is gradually freed of foreign influences, though we cannot expect to see the exuberant Italian and Flemish art toned down overnight, and it is a singularly interesting fact that Philippe Caffieri, Neapolitan by birth but naturalised in about 1665, continued to work at the Gobelins right until his death; also that at the beginning of the eighteenth century Domenico Cucci, born at Todi, was still making cabinets which were really more Italian than French in character. We even discover through the various palace accounts that, in his capacity as *ébéniste du Roi*, the Dutchman Jean Oppenord had apartments in the Louvre. Under Lebrun's ruling influence these artists of such vastly different temperaments became the skilled interpreters of a perfectly harmonious official art. Those who were artists in wood, both Frenchmen and foreigners, simplified the lines of their furniture and pruned down the turgid, confused ornamentation of the preceding period so thoroughly that the characteristics of Louis XIV furniture are identical with those of all classical art: it is majestic, sumptuous and extravagant but at the same time its proportions are well balanced and its form well defined.

The artists working at the Gobelins or the Louvre *ateliers* made furniture for the King and his Court. Although most of this furniture has been lost, we still have some very precise records in admiring contemporary descriptions, *ornemanistes'* designs and odd fragments from archives (in particular the *Journal du Garde-Meuble*, produced in its first version from 1663 and maintained regularly after 1685).

XVI *Commode, Louis XV*

It is much more difficult on the other hand to discover how ordinary individuals were in the habit of furnishing their homes; there is no document comparable to Bosse's engravings which throws any light on the matter. Museums have been slow to make collections of this humbler type of furniture, and the date and authenticity of those specimens which have been preserved are often dubious. Nevertheless we can take it for granted that from the seventeenth century onwards the general run of furniture, especially that produced in provincial workshops, continued with the decorative motifs of the previous age. For instance, it is not uncommon for an *armoire* made in mid-eighteenth century to have a Louis XIV style of carved decoration.

1 | The Techniques

The Louis XIV period is not one of innovations; it is one when established processes are perfected and generalised.

▶ *Wood*

Veneering (see Chap. I, p. 26) becomes common practice. Under Louis XIII only ebony was used for veneering, but under Louis XIV we find veneers in all kinds of precious woods, though the layers are much thinner by comparison.

Marquetry (see Chap. I, p. 31) reaches a degree of technical perfection that has never been surpassed. The range of materials employed is more or less the same as in the previous period. Yet there does seem to be a tendency to experiment with colour and this is further exploited during the course of the next century; for example, almond and box are used for yellow, holly for white, certain types of pearwood for red, walnut for brown, mahaleb cherry for pinkish-grey, etc. Boulle himself tried his hand at this coloured wood marquetry, but the true glory of the seventeenth century lies in his brass, pewter and tortoise-shell marquetry (see Frontispiece). Boulle was so successful that furniture decorated with this style of marquetry is often called 'Boulle' furniture, regardless of its maker or its date. Boulle also followed the current

xvii *Commode, Transitional*

practice of mixing bone, ivory, mother-of-pearl and transparent layers of horn painted on the underside, and this enabled him to vary the range of colours hitherto obtained. His own invention consists chiefly in glueing a sheet of tortoise-shell on to a sheet of brass and cutting them out together (i.e. their shape is identical in a pre-determined pattern). When the layers are taken apart, the twin pieces of shell and brass can be fitted into each other with perfect precision, like the different parts of a jig-saw puzzle. This great *ébéniste* owed his success to his accuracy in assembling the pieces. He would obtain two panels with exactly the same design but in one the background would be shell and the pattern brass – this was called *première partie* or first-part marquetry – and in the other the background would be brass and the pattern shell – this was called *contrepartie* or counterpart marquetry. Two pieces of furniture with identical carcases could be made but one would have *première partie* marquetry and the other *contrepartie*, alternatively this marquetry could appear on two symmetrical parts of the same piece (e.g. two doors of the same cupboard). This highly skilled technique had a grave disadvantage : veneering, which entails laying thin sheets of wood on to a cheap carcase over a relatively large surface area, is a process that renders furniture somewhat fragile in the first place ; Boulle's type of marquetry is even more delicate because it entails laying materials of a totally different nature on to wood : metals for instance (silver, brass, pewter) or animal products (bone, ivory, tortoise-shell), and what is more, the pieces inlaid are minute. Needless to say, all these multifarious materials react differently to variations in temperature and humidity and the pieces frequently come unstuck as a result. Furniture made by Boulle or his pupils has therefore been subjected to many clumsy attempts at restoration down the ages. Mention is made of these repairs as early as the end of Louis XIV's reign, but the period that proved most fatal was Louis-Philippe's reign when, under cover of 'restoration', the craze for this style resulted in drastic alterations to decoration and even to structure.

▶ *Bronze*

Boulle had himself done much to compensate for the fragility of his marquetry by fixing bronze mounts, chased and gilt, on to the more exposed parts of the furniture: bas-reliefs, medallions, friezes of classical inspiration or masks with coronas set in the middle of panels, help to keep the marquetry in position; keyhole plates or handles anchored by large mounts protect the furniture at points where it is most often touched; pendants, corner-plates and cornices prevent the edges from getting knocked. Even the legs are often cased in protective bronze mounts.

Boulle himself often modelled the bronze mounts with which he embellished his furniture and he supervised their manufacture. He was a great collector and accumulated a whole series of casts taken from masterpieces of ancient classical art that often seem to have inspired him. Nor did he think it beneath him to make *maquettes* (see Glossary) of his furniture; during his lifetime Mariette published a collection of his furniture and bronze designs, but he usually took his inspiration from the work of *ornemanistes* and more particularly from Jean Bérain.

Furniture produced by Boulle's *atelier* has an undeniable quality of richness; it is highly typical of this era of sumptuous display and grandeur, but its general outline is always clearly defined, and despite the gorgeous bronze trappings it is not overcharged. If our estimation of this great *ébéniste* has been lowered in any way it is the fault of his imitators. His sons carried on his work and in their own *ateliers* trained imitators who were still making 'Boulle' furniture as late as the mid-eighteenth century. Delaître, Montigny and Levasseur slavishly copied their master without making any innovations at a time when fashionable taste had already progressed and did more to discredit him than enhance his reputation.

▶ *Gilt Wood*

Not all furniture was overlaid with veneer or marquetry. Solid wood was still extensively used but from the early years of the century a certain *modus vivendi* began to be established within the Corporation: a distinction was drawn between artists who worked in solid wood, called '*menuisiers en bois*', and those who worked with veneers and marquetry, called '*menuisiers en ébène*' – ebony being the foremost exotic wood in frequent use (see Chap. IV, p. 74).

The role of the *menuisier en bois* is still an important one in the Louis XIV period. *Buffets*, cupboards and seat furniture are mostly made in solid wood, moulded and carved. On some pieces, however, there is a growing tendency to cover wood with gold or silver instead of leaving it plain. Wood gilding was not a new technique. It had been known since the fourteenth century but was not generally applied to furniture before mid-seventeenth century. This is easily explained: the *maître ornemaniste* would design his stucco panelling and *console* table as an *ensemble* and they would of necessity have to match. If the stucco was touched up with gilt the *console* had to have some gilt decoration too. Tables, *guéridons* and even seats, although they were not placed directly against the wall panelling, would have spoilt the harmony of the suite if they had been left in unfinished wood. The sumptuary laws prohibiting the use of gold on furniture, as well as cloth and tapestries, were re-enacted several times but with little effect. The occupants of humbler abodes often had to be content with painted wooden seats.

▶ *Solid Gold and Silver*

Finally another Corporation was called on for a short time to participate in the making of furniture: this was the Corporation of goldsmiths. It is interesting to note that it was not the first time this Corporation had intervened in the history of furniture, for had not the Dagobert faldstool come from goldsmiths' *ateliers*? Under Louis XIV not only was the King's throne made in solid silver, but countless tables, *guéridons*, sconces for girandoles and orange tree tubs. Among the various furniture artisans, we should also mention goldsmiths like the Ballins (especially Claude I, 1614–78).

Unfortunately not a vestige of these exceptional pieces has come down to us, apart from the *ornemanistes'* sketches, since they were sent back to the foundry to be melted down some time between 1790 and 1795.

▶ *Lacquer*

Lacquer was the sole technical innovation of the century (see Chap. I, p. 36). Ever since Louis XIV came to the throne, art-loving circles had been so smitten with a vogue for imported Chinese and Japanese objects (furniture, fabrics, porcelain) that it occurred to French artisans to use panels of lacquer for decorating their furniture. Since they knew nothing of the secrets of lacquer manufacture, they made the best of the situation by breaking up cabinets and screens imported from the Far East and distributing the fragments on pieces of furniture. The panels were generally planed down to make them thinner and the *ébéniste* would camouflage the inevitable splintering at the edges with bronze surrounds. Arrangements may also have been made to send panels already cut to the right size for furniture currently under construction to the Far East, so that they could be lacquered there. In any case delivery delays were long drawn out and the cost price was exorbitant.

French artisans soon tried making varnishes similar to those used by the Chinese and Japanese. Furniture varnished in this way was called 'Chinese style'. It was not until the early eighteenth century, though, that a 'Chinese' *atelier* was set up at the Gobelins and panels of lacquer, either imported or made in France, became a customary feature on furniture. Nevertheless, credit for this new decorative process must go to the Louis XIV period.

2 | Decoration and Structure

Classical antiquity as interpreted by the Italians was the main source of inspiration for the Renaissance. In the seventeenth century, French artists still have recourse to antiquity for their basic ornamentation, but they show a preference for Latin antiquity which affords them a code of aesthetics more in line with their own artistic sensibility.

Thus, through his direct contact with Roman monuments, Lebrun brought a style of decoration back to France that was both majestic and clearly defined, a complete reversal of the wild fantasies of the Renaissance artists.

One of the fundamental laws of ancient classical decoration is symmetry. This symmetry is one of the most rigidly observed rules of Louis XIV decoration; and it applies to horizontal as well as vertical axes. By and large decoration consists of the same elements as it did under the Renaissance, since the sources are the same, but the interpretation of classic themes is less fanciful. Whereas in the sixteenth century a mascaron or a lion's head could have been carved in a thousand different ways, in the seventeenth century the artist is faced with what is tantamount to an official, though not entirely stereotyped, style, laid down by the designer. The smallest ornament would be studied, carefully worked out and perfectly executed, but the artist's personal inclinations would have to be quashed in favour of the designer's conception of the scheme as a whole. This procedure results in a certain stiffness and monotony.

In Louis XIV decoration therefore we find the entire stock of motifs employed by the ancients. From the animal kingdom we get lions' heads and paws, rams' heads and horns, stags' hoofs, dolphins, griffons, sea-horses, etc.; from the vegetable kingdom we get waterlily leaves, laurels, oak and acanthus leaves, and hardly identifiable fruit and flowers. Coats of arms, trophies and mythological attributes complete the picture.

By contrast, motifs borrowed from architecture come to be used more sparingly and although we still see plenty of dentils, triglyphs and modillions, columns vanish, leaving behind only flutes as a memento of their former existence.

Certain motifs, however, come to the fore in Louis XIV ornamentation: these are mascarons and masks, especially masks encircled by sunbursts (emblem of the King), a hundred different versions of shells seen from inside or outside or with curled edges, diaper or lozenge patterns enclosing small blossoms; the lozenges or squares may be bordered by intertwining bands or strapwork: this was a common motif in parquetry.

In summing up, we have nothing truly original here: the

carved motifs lose their original vitality through being standardized and we turn to marquetry for our most lavish form of decoration.

Louis XIV furniture is therefore much more interesting from the point of view of its structure than from its decoration. Although furniture of this period is gradually becoming independent from the long-standing influence of its guardian – architecture – it keeps its fundamentally architectural form, with a tendency to the monumental since it now has to conform to a society that takes grandeur as its creed. Symmetry, observed just as rigorously in structure as in decoration, contributes to this overall effect of impersonal majesty which was the aim of all branches of art.

There are still many straight lines to be seen but they are not as rigid as they were under Louis XIII; various motifs, garlands of flowers or tassels, do much to soften the hard straight line of a seat traverse or a *bas d'armoire*. Right angles are seldom rounded off or evaded, but the slightly severe, compact appearance they give to furniture is corrected by the addition of rich bronze accessories.

Curves are adopted. These are firm, well-controlled, short sweeps that have not yet developed into the graceful, languorous Louis XV curves; on certain pieces, notably seats and *consoles*, they counterbalance the austere, majestic monotony of straight lines.

This very compact structural form is accentuated on solid wood furniture by a high relief moulding which, when the century opened, was still heavy and complex; but unlike that of the Renaissance period, this moulding is never extraneous; and, far from weakening it, it actually emphasises the majestic structure of the piece (see Plate VII).

3 | The Different Types of Furniture

▶ *Large Pieces – Armoires (wardrobes), Consoles, Bureaux*

The French word *armoire* brings to mind first of all those magnificent wardrobes by Boulle, covered with tortoise-shell and brass marquetry, which are highly prized museum pieces.

However, there were some less ambitious types of wardrobe made in solid wood, having two doors decorated with a great variety of large panels. These wardrobes are exceedingly rare; they were not part of the aristocratic furniture of that time, neither did they stand in a room or a gallery – their place was in the closet. Their contemporaries did not consider them particularly interesting and we have banned them from our modern flats because of their vast size.

The commode or chest of drawers is one of the most interesting creations of the period. Until then household linen had been stored in simple chests. During the sixteenth century, however, the introduction of cabinets had proved how useful drawers were. French craftsmen then had the idea of making large drawers in their chests that had a permanently fixed top and were raised on four feet. Boulle, indeed, may have been the inventor of this piece of furniture. In any case it was already in existence by about 1694 although the first time its name was recorded was in 1708. Boulle's commodes take the form of two long drawers, and in shape they resemble an antique sarcophagus, hence the name '*commode en tombeau*'.

This first model was quick to develop further and it assumed a standard form by the end of the century: feet are short and sturdy, uprights are tailed into a carcase deeply recessed to take two or four drawers. Handles, keyhole plates, pendants and shoes are in gilt bronze – all these are part of the general decoration.

The two types of bureau continue to exist side by side. The state bureau of the Louis XIV period is the *bureau plat* or writing-table; its frieze contains three drawers, the middle one slightly recessed. It was Boulle who established the type and even though the seventeenth-century bureau is seldom decorated with the traditional brass and tortoise-shell, its structural form at least is perpetuated.

At the same time there were bureaux of a more severe, massive appearance incorporating a set of drawers on either side of the writer and one drawer in the middle, recessed from

XVIII *Arm-Chair, Louis XVI*

the general plumb of the façade. Each set of drawers rests on four baluster or console legs, usually joined by cross-stretchers. Boulle also tried his hand at this kind of bureau.

In more modest surroundings the *bureau plat* was replaced by small, simple tables (say 2 feet 10 inches long, 1 foot 8 inches deep, 2 feet 6 inches high) standing on four curved legs. The flat top, like that of the *bureau plat*, was surrounded by an ovolo moulded brass border and the frieze adorned with marquetry. These light pieces might also have the addition of a shelf for filing papers.

▶ *Tables and Consoles*

Tables were beyond any doubt the most successful items of furniture during the '*grand siècle*': they grew ever more resplendent as the years went by. There were round, square or even pentagonal tables for special games, and tables in marble, porphyry, ebony or gilt bronze, but the ones most representative of the era are rectangular, solid wood and gilt. Their ornamentation is lavish in the extreme. The friezes are enriched with profusely carved 'aprons' resembling gold filigree work, jet cast and with the detail brought out by delicate chasing. The wood seems to have been treated like some kind of malleable material – as if it could be holed and pierced over and over again regardless of whether it would stay firm. Legs were the subject of tremendous researches into form. Although many were simple baluster legs, we sometimes find caryatids or female busts terminating in volutes supporting the heavy tops. It is on this type of furniture that we first see S-shaped legs, or curve and counter-curve merging into one continuous movement.

Two consequences arise from those gloriously ornate legs: firstly, heavier pieces have to have strong cross-stretchers – an X-shaped cross terminating in volutes fastened at the extremities by a clamp is the usual method of consolidation – and secondly, as tables were still awkward to move about, it became the custom to place them against a wall, and the decoration on one of the longest sides was therefore hidden.

Eventually, legs were simplified; once tables had been

xix *Secretaire, Louis XVI*

relegated to the wall, there was no need for them to comply with the laws of balance and so the back legs disappeared; then they were called '*console* tables' or better still '*consoles d'applique*' – even quite simply '*consoles*'. One of the most attractive kinds of *console d'applique* is that where the two curved legs meet at the centre.

▶ *Seat Furniture*

At Court, the use of seats was strictly dictated by etiquette; it is something of a surprise for example when we note that there were over thirteen hundred *tabourets* (stools) or *ployants* folding-stools) at Versailles; the Sovereign was virtually the only person entitled to sit in an arm-chair. The arm-chair remains as a seat of honour in town life but becomes more widely used by about 1640. The Louis XIV arm-chair (see Plate VIII) has a high, rectangular back completely covered in upholstery, leaving no wood showing at all; the arm-rests are still wooden, deeply curved and terminating in massive scrolls, often adorned with acanthus leaves; arm-pads come in at the end of the century. The square seat is supported by carved or moulded legs, balusters, terminal figures or consoles. These seats are so huge and heavy that they would fall to pieces if their legs were not strongly joined. H-form stretchers are the simplest; but X-form ones provide possibilities for more advanced decoration: four confronted scrolls are linked at the centre by a richly carved motif. The *chaise* differs from the *fauteuil* only in that it has no arms.

In about 1673 the *fauteuil de commodité* or 'confessional chair' made its appearance. This seat is exempt from rules of social precedence. Two stuffed, half-moon shapes called 'ears' (*oreilles*) project at right angles from the top of its high back, one on either side, for resting one's head on. The seat is normally supplied with a detachable square cushion (*carreau*).

Towards mid-century the '*canopé*' or '*canapé*' (settee) also appears. This is a particularly wide arm-chair, six or eight feet wide, made so that several people can sit on it at the same time. It looks as though two or three arm-chairs had been put together.

There is still not a great variety of furniture in the Louis XIV period but its sturdy form, sumptuous decoration and adherence to good proportion make it eminently characteristic of French society in the second half of the seventeenth century.

CHAPTER SIX

REGENCY AND LOUIS XV |

With the eighteenth century we come to the golden age of French furniture. Other countries were quick to recognise this supremacy; foreign rulers and princes (Catherine II, the Elector of Bavaria, etc.) placed orders with Parisian *ébénistes* to furnish their castles and palaces; foreign artisans (such as the Swede, G. Haupt) served their apprenticeship in French *ateliers*; and last but not least a great number of *ébénistes*, chiefly Germans, settled in Paris and asked the Corporation to give them the official title of '*maître*'. Of these J. F. Oeben (1761), Riesener (1768) and Weisweiler (1778) were all German; P. H. Mewesen (1766) was a Scandinavian; and there were many others.

However, this was not a century when the art of furniture-making was destined to be static – far from it. While the ageing king was growing still more aged and melancholy in the cold formality of his palace at Versailles, the decorative arts were beginning to shed the heavy yoke of Louis XIV decoration under the impetus of a rising new society. From 1700 to 1730 decoration becomes imperceptibly lighter, straight lines begin to be curved, and by about 1730–5 a new style is born: the Louis XV style, heralding the triumph of asymmetry and graceful, sinuous lines. A period of stability such as this was not to last long, however: from 1765 onwards we may spot the first signs of a new development creeping into decoration and form. In about 1775 lines straighten out and decoration is again directly inspired by antiquity. The

xx *Bureau, Louis XVI*

pause from 1775 to 1790 corresponds to what we call the Louis XVI style, despite the fact that no sovereign was ever less responsible for any style than this puppet king. Although the Revolution swept all royalty out of the way, it also claimed to revive the decorative arts: however there was no more of a break this time than there had been before. The development that occurred between 1790 and 1804 is hardly noticeable and the *Directoire* is the most difficult of all styles to pin down.

Thus we have two relatively stable periods, 1735–65 (Louis XV) and 1775–90 (Louis XVI), spaced in between periods of flux that have been given the arbitrary names of Regency (1700–35), Transition (1765–75) and *Directoire* (1790–1804). It is difficult to ascertain dates of intermediate styles exactly, or to give them names, but, in order to understand the transition from one style to another, we should study one of the most characteristic phases of these periods, when art is at a turning-point between two styles. We should also add that the above dates are valid only as far as Paris is concerned. Development was considerably slower in the provinces: there the Regency style continued in fashion right up to about 1740 and the Louis XVI style was still very popular in the early nineteenth century.

1 | Formation of the Louis XV Style: The Regency Period

Philippe d'Orléans' effective rule lasted eight years (1715–23) but in art the so-called Regency period extends over thirty years (1700–30).

We can see the first hints of a change in ornamental style as far back as 1690, the year Lebrun died. The leading fashionable designer round about 1690 is Jean I. Bérain. His highly architectural compositions and perfect symmetry bring him well in line with the purest classical tradition, but a certain light fantastic touch creeps into his details: *chinoiseries* and *singeries* (monkey-pieces) make their first appearance. Bérain had a direct influence on furniture, since A. C. Boulle was often inspired by his designs.

XXI *Bonheur-du-Jour, Louis XVI*

G

From about 1700 onwards a new society addicted to pleasure grew up around Philippe d'Orléans at the Palais Royal and the Duchesse du Maine at Sceaux; the purpose of this society's existence was no longer florid magnificence and formal grandeur but light amusement and personal comfort. From this time onwards the king is by no means the only person to order furniture; young noblemen or rich bourgeois also want to furnish their homes in the latest fashion. *Menuisiers* and *ébénistes* are therefore obliged to adapt themselves in order to please their new clients.

► *Decoration and Structure*

We might sum up the Regency style by saying that it is the transition from a rectilinear style to a curvilinear one, for we cannot say that any particular line or ornament is a unique feature of the Regency style. All the Regency elements are either modified Louis XIV motifs or Louis XV elements in embryo. A Regency piece contains elements borrowed from both styles – juxtaposed but in harmony.

The hyper-strict symmetry that prevailed under Louis XIV tends to become less rigid. Horizontally, symmetry is still scrupulously observed, but vertically it is often disregarded. In spite of this we are still nowhere near the deliberate asymmetry of the *rocaille* or Rococo style. Structure is still solid and heavy but the straight lines are made to appear softer; dainty trails of foliage – twining convolvulus plants and twigs that branch out from uprights – break up the severe structural form. The corners of square frames are disguised by being scooped away, or decorated with shells and flowers. Decoration becomes lighter, elegantly attenuated and supple – in fact, less formal. The shape of the shell changes; it is no longer fat and bulbous, its edges are jagged and occasionally it is even pierced. Waterlily leaves and acanthus leaves undergo the same treatment. Leaves in general are lighter and less obtrusive. We can now begin to appreciate the beauty of smooth, flat surfaces framed with ornamentation. Mascarons, no doubt considered too clumsy, are few and far between. Lozenges or diaper patterns enclosing small blossoms are still used but occasionally they are distorted: the sides of the lozenge or square bulge outwards. The formerly heroic attributes mellow into more human scenes – favourite themes are hunting and fishing instead of war. Finally, the Far East (China, Persia, India) provides a source of light-hearted motifs (dragons, parasols, peacock feathers, weirdly-shaped rocks, etc.), all in keeping with the fashionable taste of the times.

▶ *The Different Types of Furniture*

Seats are the first to show signs of change. In the newly established society, formal etiquette is abandoned in favour of conversational entertainment. The Louis XIV style of high-backed arm-chair is no longer suitable; it rapidly becomes lighter and easier to handle; the back is made lower, the wooden framework becomes visible again and the traverse at the top of the back is arched. Stretchers tend to disappear, but where they are retained they are reduced to two cross-pieces in X-formation, with a very restrained moulding. Arms are set back and follow a generous curve outwards so that ladies may sit down comfortably in those panniered skirts which came into fashion in about 1718. However, the uprights of the back are still straight and the square seat stays until approximately 1720. It goes without saying that a Regency arm-chair does not necessarily incorporate all these modifications; for example, the wooden back may be quite plain but the legs may still be laden with cumbersome cross-stretchers.

We also see a rapid development in tables, with the exception of consoles, which, being directly related to the wall decorations, still preserve a heavy Louis XIV richness and splendour for a short time. Free-standing tables, on the other hand, lose their cross-stretchers, and baluster and pedestal legs become less frequent – straight lines are on the way out. Preference is given to cabriole legs with a double bend making an elongated S-shape, or scroll legs, also known as *pied-de-biche* ('hoofed' foot). In the previous period the *pied-de-biche* almost invariably terminated in the hoof of what was intended to be the hind leg of a doe, but during the

Regency the *pied-de-biche* usually terminates in a volute resting on a small wooden cube.

Regency commodes (see Plate ix) are extremely interesting and typical of this ambiguous style. They are still massive and heavy and their two sections are still generally very distinct, yet straight lines have almost completely vanished; the legs are cabriole, the lower traverse of the body also dips in a curve – Cressent is believed to have introduced the double curved or crossbow-shaped profile – and even the sides of the seat swell outwards. Precious wood veneers and sumptuous bronze accessories add to the extreme elegance of this furniture.

We know that some of the Regency *armoires* were also very fine, especially one in the *Musée Jacquemart-André* and another, attributed to Cressent, in the *Musée des Arts Décoratifs*. These two pieces are good examples of the trend in furniture over a period of about thirty years. After the sombre ebony and tortoise-shell backgrounds of Boulle's *armoires*, Regency *armoires* with their colourful veneers of exotic wood come as a complete change; instead of heavy, elaborate bronze fittings spread-eagled across the centre of panels, we see a marked preference for a light, elegant cross-banding used to frame doors and enhance the beauty of the veneer. Lastly, even the hard, rectilinear structure softens: the sides of the carcase and doors are slightly and gracefully bowed.

It is not so easy to pick out specifically Regency characteristics in other categories of furniture. A new type of bronze mount may be our only indication that a certain piece is Regency and not Louis XIV. For example, under Louis XIV acanthus leaves might be carefully draped to form a pendant on the corners of a *bureau plat*; under the Regency the elements of decoration are still basically the same but they are treated in a different way; they might for example take the form of weirdly grimacing dragons or elegant female busts. Cressent, who was the *ébéniste du Régent*, made a speciality of the delicately profiled type of Spanish female head called an *espagnolette*.

The hybrid nature of Regency furniture is not without a certain charm, but this period is more interesting for its promises of things to come than for any outstanding pieces it produced.

During these thirty years of experimentation, furniture artisans gained complete mastery of the techniques that were to be the glory of the next period (veneering, marquetry, bronze-work); they explored the possibilities of curved lines in structural form as well as in decoration. They also succeeded in capturing a wealthy clientèle's interest in their products; as from this time all interiors, however modest their pretensions to luxurious living, boasted some elegant furniture in the latest fashion.

2 | Louis XV

Round about 1730–5 certain new techniques were tried out and put into practice. A choice of decorative forms grew up. For close on thirty years there was no apparent need for fresh outbursts of invention, and although we find that many artisans used to co-operate on one and the same piece, and that there were strong differences between individual temperaments, the general output of the Parisian *menuisiers* and *ébénistes* from 1730 to 1760/5 was remarkably consistent.

3 | The Techniques

One of the eighteenth-century *maîtres menuisiers*, André-Jacob Roubo (1739–91), made a minutely detailed description of the tools and procedure necessary for furniture manufacture; it entails six folio volumes illustrated with numerous plates which he himself designed and engraved (*L'art du Menuisier*, 1768–75). Roubo's criticisms are probably over-harsh and prejudiced, rooted as they must have been in inevitable professional rivalries, but it is none the less true that such evidence supplied by an eighteenth-century furniture specialist is of immense value to us.

▶ *Wood (solid wood, veneering, marquetry)*

Woods used by *menuisiers* are native woods. Oak is used relatively little, though there are some fine *armoires* or *buffets* made in solid oak (see Plate xi), and after 1760 the carcases of some exquisite pieces were also oak. Beech was the commonest wood for seat furniture; some *menuisiers* also used walnut and lime, and common white wood (pine, poplar) served as a carcase for most works of *ébénisterie*.

As in previous periods, the provincial *menuisiers* tend to use woods from their native district. Thus we find furniture in olive, cherry, pear, chestnut and service-tree. *Ebénistes* on the other hand use chiefly imported woods. Our information on these woods is very scant: the typical eighteenth-century *ébéniste* is not concerned with their origins, let alone their scientific names. The only things that interest him are colour and grain. There are endless references to tulipwood (yellow streaked with red), purplewood (purplish brown), satinwood (red satinwood = red with yellow markings; yellow satinwood = figured golden yellow) Mahaleb cherrywood (rose-tinted grey), etc., but no proper names are ever given that would indicate their botanical origins. The top of a small Latz table reproduced (Plate xiv) is a good example of the effects that *ébénistes* were able to achieve by using coloured woods. The musical instrument stands out against a background of tulipwood and satinwood, the borders are in purplewood. Roubo quotes about fifty different woods, but the origins he gives are often questionable. Typical of his trade, he attaches more importance to subtle nuances of colour than to accurate names. The colours are lost on us to some extent, since wood becomes discoloured after being exposed to the air for any length of time; the only way we can get some idea of the brilliant polychromy of eighteenth-century furniture is to look at restorations which reveal sections of marquetry normally covered by bronze fittings, or internal panels. For instance, we find that the purple in purplewood tends to become brown and the yellow and red streaks in tulipwood turn into a uniform honey-gold. The *ébéniste* keeps to ebony for his detailed marquetry and is not above using native woods such as holly, yew, box and barberry.

The two current techniques in exotic wood are veneering and marquetry (see Chap. I, p. 32). Neither of these is new, but the eighteenth-century *ébéniste* has to grapple with a fresh problem unknown to his predecessors: glueing his veneers and marquetry designs on to curved surfaces. For either process he cuts the fancy wood with the grain, to a thickness of two or three millimetres. Then it is classified according to its colour and grain. When he wants to get a perfectly continuous surface pattern, the *ébéniste* concentrates on disguising the joins between the leaves of veneer and selecting his wood so that the grain matches well.

From the so-called process of veneering – which entails covering a relatively large surface area with thin sheets of wood – we come, almost without noticing the transition, to that process known as marquetry, which is different in that the pieces of fancy wood used tend to be very small, very varied and very numerous, and they follow a predetermined pattern. The more complicated the pattern, the more varied the small pieces of wood and the more difficult the whole operation becomes. The *ébéniste* therefore has an almost unlimited number of combinations at his disposal with which he can decorate his furniture. It is still called veneering, or to be more precise cross-banding, when the *ébéniste* simply lays his large sheets of wood with the grain or tones in opposite directions; he may for instance place his bands horizontally, vertically or obliquely. Veneering also applies to large geometrical patterns (i.e. sunbursts, stars, lozenges) decorating an entire panel, but we reach the borderline between veneering and marquetry when we come to the more or less complicated versions of rosettes and four- or five-point stars. If, instead of spreading over the whole area of a panel, a five-point star is repeated several times on the same panel, it will of course have to be made up of many small pieces of wood: in that case we call it marquetry. Four-point stars, rosettes, and tiny blossoms are often inscribed in circles, squares, lozenges or rectangles. We can find every conceivable geometrical figure: diaper, check, herring-bone, etc. Imitation basket-work also enjoys a great vogue.

However, the skill of the *maîtres-ébénistes* does not end there. They want to try reproducing real pictures. The simplest of these compositions take the form of utensils such as teapots, teacups, vases, ewers, etc. – more or less in direct imitation of Chinese models. These objects may also be given a three-dimensional effect by way of variation (see Plate xɪɪ); in such instances the wood can be shaded by different methods; by scratching it with a burin, or by dipping it in acid or hot sand. Composite motifs demand far more skill on the part of the artisan. We already find some of the best quality furniture decorated with cunningly intertwined garden implements or hunting or musical trophies (see Plate xɪv), but there is no doubt about it that floral motifs demand the most advanced knowledge of marquetry techniques. At the beginning of the Louis XV period some *ébénistes* like Lacroix started to specialise in this form of decoration, but the most brilliantly successful pieces did not appear until the next period, from the hands of masters like Riesener. The simpler designs show sprays of flowers trailing gracefully across the whole area of a panel (see Plate xxv), but they become more intricate when we add some fruit hanging from the branches, or a few birds perched here and there. In other instances the floral motif might be confined to the centre of the panel: branches and bouquets of flowers sprout from wicker-work baskets or vases. Very occasionally we may come across scenes with little figures (see Glossary), but these only appear on furniture made by foreign *ébénistes*, newly arrived in France. Wolf and Roentgen for instance were admitted as *maîtres* to the Parisian Guild, but the fact remains that they had been trained in the German and not the French school. For designs like those quoted above, where the pictures require an exceptional variety of colours, the *ébéniste* is obliged to extend the range he can obtain from natural woods. He can achieve this to a considerable extent by using wood dyes. There is nothing new about this technique but the eighteenth-century *ébénistes* were particularly good at it. In this way they could get a great variety of blue, red, grey or yellow tones. Needless to say, polychrome dyed wood does not stay bright for long, and it is rare indeed to find a piece of furniture today on which we can still see and appraise the sumptuously rich effect of these dyes.

Panels of veneer or marquetry are often framed by one,

xxɪɪ *Armoire, Louis XV*

two or three fillets of a different variety of wood, or even of the same variety but cut across the grain. Ebony, satinwood, holly and barberry are used mainly for this purpose.

This brief list of marquetry designs may give us some idea of the lengths to which *ébénistes* of the Louis XV period went in order to keep their art alive and progressive. Delicately tinted floral compositions were clearly used only on show pieces, ordered mostly by the king and his entourage. For their normal production *ébénistes* were content to use the geometrical type of marquetry design.

▶ *Tortoise-shell, Mother-of-pearl and Brass*

The Louis XV period is so strongly associated with coloured wood marquetry that we are inclined to forget that towards the end of the century tortoise-shell, mother-of-pearl and brass marquetry also enjoyed a certain vogue. We might well think *ébénistes* like Delaître (*maître* in 1738), Montigny (*maître* in 1766), Levasseur (*maître* in 1767) and Lemarchand (*maître* in 1789), to mention only the most famous, were retrograde; but their mid-eighteenth-century work should certainly not be overlooked. It also prolongs the influence of that great Louis XIV *ébéniste* whose youngest son, Charles-Joseph Boulle, did not die until 1754. This technique was kept up for another good reason; the *meubles de la Couronne* made by A.-C. Boulle were always needing repair – in the Louis XV period Levasseur was one of those called on for this type of work.

▶ *Lacquers*

We have already seen that we owe the introduction of this decorative process to the Louis XIV period. Under Louis XV it becomes common practice and the *vernisseurs'* greatest triumph was to become independent of Far Eastern models and create a uniquely French style in lacquer work (see page 36).

Yet even when the French had managed to achieve a considerable mastery of the technique, the fashion for imported lacquers still lingered on. Japanese lacquers were the most highly prized (see Plate xxviii). Persons of taste in the eighteenth century liked their grace and harmony of composition, variety of theme and glittering gold highlights. There are some red and vermilion lacquers, but black backgrounds are most common. The panels are painted with landscapes: soft moonlight over hills and temples, golden ripples across marshlands, rivers splashing over rocks or winding their way under hump-backed bridges. Trees (pines, birches, bamboos), flowers (water-lilies, chrysanthemums) and plants (reeds, ferns) complete the background, and figures (horsemen, fishermen in a boat, poets meditating on a rock) give life to the natural scene. Chinese lacquers (see Plate xxii) are often more cluttered in design though their subjects are the same. Lastly we have Coromandel lacquers, which are really Chinese in origin and which are made in an entirely different fashion: the design is etched and dug out in the generally black surface of the lacquer: these hollows are then filled with various other brightly coloured lacquers. Coromandel lacquers are therefore very easy to recognise; their tones are quite different from the warm, mellow tones of other types of lacquer – only obtained by applying coat after coat of gum. The rich polychromy of Coromandel lacquers, obtained by juxtaposition of brilliant colours, lends itself well to flower and shell motifs and birds with shimmering, multi-coloured plumage. Their design is often over-crowded and they do not have the harmony or the mellow quality found in Japanese lacquers. We can manage to tell the genuine from the pseudo-Oriental lacquers, so common in all Louis XV decoration, by details of costume or the general graceful air of certain plants (particularly bamboos), but even then it is difficult to be sure.

However, the black background which fitted in so well with ebony furniture did not harmonise with the lighter tones of Louis XV decor. The best French *vernisseurs*, such as the Martin brothers, took it upon themselves to invent lacquers with light, gay backgrounds which in no time were a great success, especially at Court. These *vernisseurs* stopped making imitations of the Far East and, with the aid of pure transparent French varnishes, filled the panels of their furniture with delightfully dainty little painted figures, copied from the work of fashionable artists like Boucher, Teniers or Greuze. French artisans had once more succeeded in freeing themselves from the bondage of imitation and had transformed a foreign technique into part of their national heritage.

▶ *Bronze Mounts*

Bronze accessories, which were first brought into fashion under the Regency by *ébénistes* like Cressent, became a compulsory form of decoration under Louis XV for all veneered, marquetried or lacquered furniture. Even on particularly fine pieces (see Plate xii) bronze mounts were used to a limited extent. In these instances bronze keeps its original function of protecting the fragile marquetry from knocks and blows. Only the shoes, keyhole plates and handles are in bronze, sometimes with the addition of a narrow strip running along the edges and accentuating the general contour of the piece. On the other hand, some pieces are encased in what is virtually a bronze strait-jacket: not only are the friezes, pendants, exaggeratedly fanciful shoes, and *rocaille* work framing the edges of the piece made in bronze, but bronze even invades the centre of panels, and the beauty of the exotic wood is lost under such excessive decoration.

There was one disadvantage in such a widespread use of bronze; the cost of manufacturing mounts was very high because it involved a series of long and delicate operations (see Chap. I, p. 38). Bronze-workers would often try to economise by using the same moulds over again and supplying identical mounts for different *ébénistes* and different pieces of furniture. They also economised on gilding processes. For a long-lasting, brilliant gold, gilding should really be done with gold leaf or mercury (see Chap. I, p. 40), but as both of these processes are extremely costly, bronzeworkers would compromise by 'gilding' the general run of their mounts with a coat of ordinary varnish; in these cases the bronze soon tarnishes.

Another disadvantage is that whilst under the Regency bronze mounts were an exceptional form of decoration and were designed and made with extreme care, under Louis XV the standard of these mounts varies. The poor quality and lack of imagination in the endlessly stereotyped *passe-partout rocaille* mounts contrast oddly with the refinement and elegance of the B.V.R.B. bronze (Bernard Van Risen Burg)[1] (see Plates XIII and XXII) or the sumptuous richness of one by Riesener.

We must add, however, that a few privileged *ébénistes* such as the *ébénistes du roi*, or *maîtres* directly responsible to the Crown and thus happily exempt from the Guild's petty contentions, were allowed to disregard the rules and design, model or cast bronze mounts for their own furniture.

Some bronze-workers enjoyed a reputation every bit as great as the top-ranking *ébénistes*. Jacques Caffieri's (1678–1755) exquisitely rich bronze mounts, and those of his son Philippe III (1714–74), prove to what an amazing extent the Louis XV craftsmen had mastered this branch of art.

4 | Decoration and Structure

▶ *Decoration*

Rocaille work or Rococo is the most characteristic feature of Louis XV decoration. Two foreign designers are chiefly responsible for introducing the Rococo style into France: Juste-Aurèle Meisonnier, born in Turin, and Gilles-Marie Oppenord, the son of a Dutch cabinet-maker who had not long since adopted French nationality. Rococo art is the combination of the fantastic and the real, objects that are true to life but grouped together in a manner physically impossible: for instance we might find a whole company of monkeys, fantastic little animals, dogs and birds swinging from bows of ribbon or delicate trellis-work patterns. All these elements of decoration are caught up in one great swirling movement – they show no regard for symmetry and defy even the most elementary laws of balance. This style reached its climax after 1725 and naturally its influence was reflected in the art of furniture-making. The pieces that have come down to us are twisted and distorted in form, with

[1] The mysterious B.V.R.B. finally identified (*Connaissance des Arts*, 1957, no. 61, page 56 to 63).

heavily ornate bronze mounts that nowadays offend the Frenchman's inborn taste for clarity and balance.

However, the Rococo style soon settled down in France. The leading Louis XV *ornemaniste* who designed more models for *ébénistes* than anyone else was the French artist Nicolas Pineau. He is the man to whom credit goes for taking the whole motley collection of Rococo elements and relating them all to one ideal axis. No longer do we see a refusal to conform to a single rhythm or the deliberate unbalance between one mass and another: we now have a coherent plan underlying the decoration, composed as it is of weirdly shaped rocks, capricious little sprays and tendrils, jagged leaves curling at the edges, twisted shells, heavily draped animal pelts, distorted cartouches and exaggeratedly sinuous volutes. The more extravagant flights of fantasy have been suppressed, especially where furniture is concerned.

Rocaille is not, however, indispensable to Louis XV decoration. Floral motifs are the only ornament on a great deal of Louis XV furniture, especially seats. The flowers are generally stylised; we may find them arranged in sprays, bouquets, garlands and pendants, or scattered among stouter branches. Flower decoration is even more recurrent than *rocaille* – in marquetry designs (see Plates XVI and XXV), solid wood carving and bronze-work (see Plate X).

We could be forgiven for thinking that straight lines were altogether eliminated from Louis XV decoration, but this is not so. Compact, clear-cut geometrical marquetry patterns, as frequent as unexpected, counterbalance the languorous curves of the general silhouette and the exuberant modelling of the bronze mounts.

▶ *Structure*

The Louis XV period is the only one in which furniture is fully emancipated from the ruling influence of architecture. A single preoccupation underlies the whole structure of furniture: its adaptation to the needs of a voluptuous society dedicated entirely to material comfort and pleasure. Thus seats are moulded as far as possible into the shape of the human body. Although straight backs are still to be found, many seats are *cabriolet,* where the concave back curves comfortably round the back of a seated person (see Plate x). As a further concession to comfort, seats are also made lower, inviting a relaxed, nonchalant attitude (Louis XIV seats were 18 inches to 20 inches high; Louis XV ones 14 inches to 16 inches). *Menuisiers* took great pains to make different seats to suit every purpose, but there is one common feature amid this multiplicity of shapes: all the lines are elegantly curved or bowed. We look in vain for a straight line anywhere (see Plate x). Seats are no longer divided up into different sections: a single continuous line runs from the foot to the top of the back; the moulding on the legs is carried on into the valance without a break, and the console leg and the arm seem to be carved out of the same piece of wood.

The rest of Louis XV furniture develops in the same way as seats; façades and sides are gracefully bowed, legs are also curved (cabriole). This abhorrence of straight lines is carried so far that not even the tops of furniture are level: for example the top of a *secrétaire à abattant* (drop-front secretaire) signed by Migeon is slightly curved.

Anxious to please a sophisticated clientèle, both *ébénistes* and *menuisiers* racked their brains to create new forms of furniture that could be adapted to any purpose. They therefore produced quantities of small, light, easily mobile pieces – mutely obedient servants to their owners' every whim. Drawers, flaps and pigeon-holes were multiplied *ad lib.*; such pieces may be opened by an *abattant* (drop-front), a lid (to be lifted vertically), or one or more doors concealing a set of drawers. Some of the gaming or music tables are incredibly complicated (Migeon's *table à sextuor* at Fontainebleau is one example).

Absence of straight lines and variety of form are therefore the chief characteristics of the Louis XV period.

5 | The Different Types of Furniture

Never have furniture-makers of any period taken such a delight in the endless renewal of form. The public's taste for new conceits and the general desire for personal comfort provided powerful stimulants. The shape of each piece of furniture was carefully worked out in every detail so that all unnecessary movement or effort on the part of its owner could be eliminated. This variety and adaptability are the real reasons why Louis XV furniture remained so popular throughout two centuries.

We should note here that although furniture is extremely varied in form, there are never many pieces in one room. A Louis XV salon contains about ten pieces at the most.

▶ *Seat Furniture*

This can be divided into two categories: *sièges à la Reine* – a graceful compliment to Marie Lesczynska – where the back is flat, and *sièges en cabriolet*, where the back is concave.

The typical Louis XV arm-chair (either *en cabriolet* or *à la Reine*) has a much lower back than Louis XIV or Regency arm-chair, no higher than the shoulders of a seated person. Even the seat is not so far removed from the ground as it was in previous periods. Legs are cabriole and cross-stretchers disappear altogether. Louis XV armchairs are comfortable and easy to move about, the perfect accessory for the sophisticated life of the times (see Plate x). Other types of chair follow the same trends.

As well as the ordinary kind of arm-chair, a great number of special chairs appeared on the scene and we should be careful to get their names right. Antique dealers' jargon has made us familiar with some names which were only adopted at the end of the nineteenth century and it is difficult now to establish the correct ones.

The *bergère* is an arm-chair with a loose seat cushion and upholstered arms. It has a more obliquely sloping back than the simple arm-chair.

The *marquise* – which could perhaps more properly be called a *tête-à-tête* – is a wider and deeper form of *bergere*, big enough for two people to sit side by side.

The *fauteuil en confessional* – also known as a wing chair – already existed in the previous period. Its back is high enough to rest one's head on; the solid sides extend upwards into small round projections called *joues* or *oreilles* (wings);

the sides follow an exaggerated curve inwards at elbow level (see Plate xv).

The *fauteuil de cabinet* – nowadays we would call it a *fauteuil de bureau* or desk chair – has a very distinctive shape. The seat is semicircular at the back but has a very pronounced curve in front; the back follows the curve of the seat exactly; the legs, however, are curiously placed: there is one supporting the curved front seat rail, another at the centre-point of the back semi-circle, and the other two directly support the scrolled arm-rests on either side. There are some *fauteuils de cabinet* with five legs: these have two legs at the back. This type of seat is frequently caned or upholstered in leather.

The *fauteuil à coiffer* or dressing-table chair is often caned too; the back top rail dips down at the centre (see Glossary).

The *voyeuse* or *voyelle* (conversation chair) may be made to look like an ordinary chair or armchair; in either case it has a flat, curved top rail on which one could lean one's elbows while watching a game of cards. The seat may be the same shape as usual, but there are also certain types of *voyeuses* for men where the seat narrows towards the back, so that they could sit astride it.

The *canapé* or settee already existed under Louis XIV. Under Louis XV it shrinks to smaller dimensions (about 5 feet), generally resting on four legs at the back. It is in fact an extra wide arm-chair on which several people could sit together. The *canapé* has as many variations as the arm-chair. At the period under discussion it was a standard item of salon furniture.

One variation of the *canapé* is the *sopha* (sofa); this word came into fashion at the end of the seventeenth century along with the mania for everything Turkish. It is a *canapé* with a lower seat than normal, completely covered by upholstery.

The Louis XV period also sees an abundance of lounging chairs. The *duchesse* or *chaise longue* is a *bergère* with a seat deep enough to accommodate the legs of a seated person when stretched out. The far end of the seat might also have a back, though much lower. A *duchesse* is said to be *brisé* when the extension is formed by one, or possibly two, separate stools.

The *veilleuse* is a kind of day-bed for a lady to recline on in the same way as she would on a *duchesse*; the only difference

between the two is that the *veilleuse* has a third back joining the lower to the higher one. It was apparently the custom to have two *veilleuses* facing each other – one would have the high back on the left, and the other on the right.

The *lit de repos* was already in use in the seventeenth century. It was also called a *lit du jour* (day-bed) and is virtually a single bed that will take a person lying at full length. It may have either one or two backs.

We will end our already long list with three sorts of divans which derive their names from the East and which are only slightly different from each other:

The *ottomane* (ottoman) is a small *canapé* with an oval seat; the back follows the contours of the seat exactly and dips at the front to join up with the arm-rests. Thus the combined back and arm-rests give the impression of a single unit. The *turquoise* is a variation on the *ottomane* but with the back divided more distinctly into three sections. The *paphose* is another variation on the *ottomane*; here the seat is bean or kidney shaped and the arm-rests are practically non-existent.

▶ *Beds*

Beds can be divided into two categories: French and Polish. The French bed has just one headboard; in the eighteenth century the traditional four-poster French bed tends to disappear and be substituted by the *lit à la duchesse*; here the tester is no longer supported on four posts, but the canopy that takes its place is either suspended from the ceiling or fixed on to the wall; the lower part of the bed is therefore completely detached. This version of bed did exist in the seventeenth century but it was an exception and was called an angel bed at the time.

The Polish bed on the other hand has two or sometimes three backs. Here the posts supporting the canopy have been extended into iron rods from which graceful draperies fall. It was called a *lit à la turque* or a *lit à la chinoise* depending on how the draperies were arranged.

XXIV *Chairs, Consulate Period*

H

▶ *General Furniture*

Furniture in general becomes the monopoly of the *ébéniste*. Rarely do we find a piece of Louis XV furniture carved in solid wood. We should, however, mention several extremely fine *armoires* (most in oak) and some double-bodied *buffets* with four doors (see Plate XI). Certain console tables in gilt wood were also made by *menuisiers*; otherwise all furniture from now onwards is made by *ébénistes*.

▶ *Tables*

There are no tables designed exclusively for eating still in existence, but instead we have a great variety of small and versatile occasional tables that begin at this time to fill the salons and other rooms. Nearly all of them are veneered or decorated with marquetry. Firstly, we have a number of small tables with a vague, general function: books and miscellaneous objects would have been placed on them. They are fitted at different levels with flat shelves serving as stretchers: they can also be extended at will by front or side flaps made to slide out from under the main part of the table-top. Sometimes they have one or more drawers fitted under the table-top, or even a cupboard compartment closed in by a door. They come in so many different forms that it is impossible to describe them in detail.

Some tables, however, were made with very specific purposes in mind. These are the gaming tables; their form varies according to the game they are intended for.

There are square tables for quadrille, round tables for brelan, triangular tables for tri. Some gaming tables even have a marquetry chess-board top.

One of the most delightful creations of the eighteenth century is the *chiffonnière* which is a box mounted on four tall, slender legs (see Glossary). The box might contain two drawers opening at the front, or possibly one at the side. It could also be closed in quite simply by a door. This small, dainty, exquisitely made piece served to hold ladies' embroidery or sewing trifles. The *coiffeuse*, or rather the *toilette*, is a toilet table with the top divided into three flaps which

can be lifted up to reveal tiny compartments inside (see
Plate xii).

Writing-tables were already being made at the beginning
of the century. These are small-scale versions of the *bureau
plat*. The top is inlaid with leather or marquetry and often
contains tiny little drawers on either side.

▶ *Bureaux*

The *bureau plat* has barely changed since the previous period.
It contains three drawers, the middle one slightly recessed so
that it is easier to sit down in front of it. It was often equipped
with a small box containing shelves or pigeon-holes for filing
papers (*serre-papiers* or *cartonnier*) which could be fixed either
at the back or to one side of the table.

The *secrétaire a dos d'âne* – also called a *secrétaire en pente*
('donkey's back' or lean-to secretaire) – is a small-sized article
of furniture which, when open, combines a flat writing
surface with pigeon-holes or small drawers for one's paper.
When the lid is closed it makes an angle of 45° with the flat
top. It stands in the centre of the room and might have a
lacquer or marquetry panel decorating the back, according to
what was required. There are also a number of *secrétaires à
double pente* at which two people could sit facing each other.

The *secrétaire à abattant* (drop-front secretaire) see Plate
xxv – or *secrétaire en armoire* – is usually larger than the
secrétaire à dos d'âne. The fundamental difference is that the
drop-front closes into a vertical position. It is intended to
stand against the wall and the carcase is not veneered at the
back. The lower section contains a set of drawers often hidden
from view by doors.

▶ *Commodes*

These were cavernous and massive under the Regency, but
are now growing lighter. Until about 1740 the typical Louis
XV commode (see Plate xvi) contains only two drawers
separated by a clearly visible traverse. It rests on high,
cabriole legs. The façades and sides are gracefully bowed and
always decorated with marquetry or lacquer panels. All too

often a network of bronze *rocaille* hides the beauty of the original decoration. The *encoignure* or corner cupboard is one variation on the commode. It is in fact a small commode made to fit into the corner of a room. It is therefore triangular in shape and closed in by a curved door. *Encoignures* were made in pairs.

All Louis XV furniture stems from the examples we have described above, but the variations are practically infinite since every *ébéniste* and every furniture-dealer tried to attract customers by the unusual and original shapes of his furniture. Hence we find heart-shaped *poudreuses*, bedside tables, occasional tables, coffee tables, etc.

Grace and gaiety are the chief characteristics of Louis XV furniture. French artists contrived to avoid the incoherent, hideously tortuous forms that had resulted, east of the Rhine, from an over-conscientious adherence to Rococo ideals. Sinuous, graceful, supple lines disguise all joints in the wood and make furniture seem almost alive. Furniture of this period has its own code of æsthetics; it breaks away from all the rules, evades all set formulæ, and frees itself from every vestige of imitation, following none but the dictates of free, fanciful flights of imagination. It marks, in fact, the only time when French furniture shows a true spirit of independence and originality.

| LOUIS XVI

1 | The Formation of the Louis XVI Style: The Transitional Period

The artistic phase which we call a 'return to antiquity', and which has an effective influence on French furniture only after 1765, has much earlier origins.

The Rococo style and its exaggerated curves had reached its height in every branch of the decorative arts when Mme de Pompadour sent her brother, the future Marquis de Marigny, to Italy (1749–51) to serve his artistic apprenticeship under the aegis of the designer Cochin and the architect Soufflot. This event marks the beginning of a succession of visits to Italy for study purposes, and a great many pattern-books – reproductions of ancient Greek or Roman master-pieces – were compiled as a result. We should also mention the Comte de Caylus' *Recueil des Antiquités Egyptiennes, Etrusques, Grecques et Gauloises*, published in 1752. This was a tremendously successful work. It meant that artists and craftsmen who could not go to Italy themselves were able to keep up to date with the renewed interest in ancient Rome.

However, it was the discovery of the two buried towns of Herculaneum and Pompeii that roused the greatest enthusiasm. French artists had long been familiar with Roman and even Greek public buildings, but they had hitherto had absolutely no idea of how the ancients led their normal daily lives. Now the fanatical devotees of the ancient world suddenly find themselves gazing in wonder at private houses which reveal mural decorations, lighting systems, furniture and all manner of utensils. From 1748 onwards the shape, colour and ornamentation of this furniture, which had just been dug up from under the ashes, becomes common knowledge through the medium of widespread publications.

Nothing could have had a greater impact on furniture design than the discovery of these miscellaneous domestic objects, especially as the public was beginning to tire of the Rococo style after twenty years. In 1754 Cochin the younger published his *Supplication aux orfèvres, ciseleurs, sculpteurs en bois pour les appartements*. All of a sudden the Louis XV style is condemned for its excess of complicated curves 'which make the prettiest contortions in the world', and its abundant floral decoration – in a word, for not heeding the sweet voice of reason.

The 'return to antiquity' does, however, mean progress. Dainty little ornaments, trinkets, jewellery and goldsmith's work are the first things to be affected by this new trend; furniture 'holds out' until about 1760 or 1765. Then, after ten years and a series of modifications, the sinuous lines gradually straighten out and Rococo decoration is abandoned in favour of motifs taken from the ancient classical repertoire. The hybrid furniture composed of mixed Louis XV and Louis XVI elements and manufactured in this period is classified as the 'transitional' style.

We will now examine several pieces of furniture which will show us the progress made as regards both structure and decoration.

Bronze accessories and decoration in general are the first to show signs of change.

A transitional arm-chair for instance keeps its undulating Louis XV contours, but the seat rail is decorated with imbricated scale-work or swags of laurel. A little later on the basic structure of the seat alters: the back is still *en cabriolet* but the legs are straight – possibly fluted – and joined at right angles to the seat rail by a cubical block. That sharp division between the different sections of the seat which had disappeared in the Louis XV period, is now re-affirmed.

The same process applies to tables. A transitional table

may still rest on slightly cabriole legs, whilst the frieze may be decorated with short rows of fluting or *raies de coeur*.

Commodes (see Plate xvii) are even more interesting. In the first phase, only the bronze fittings are modified: plaques decorated with geometrical motifs form pendants; Greek-key and interlaced patterns appear on friezes. Handles, fixed under Louis XV, return to the drop type. The body of the piece becomes rectangular, but legs remain cabriole for a long time to come. *Ebénistes* now devise an ingenious method of counteracting the stark appearance of plain rectilinear surfaces: they make a slightly projecting central panel to the façade of the commode – this is called a *décrochement* or break-front.

Lastly, the creation of the *bureau à cylindre* (roll- or cylinder-top desk) is attributable to this period. The prototype is the famous *bureau du Roi*, begun by Oeben and finished by Riesener in 1769. This piece of furniture marks a step forward from the *bureau plat* fitted with a shelf on top: not only does it provide a large surface for spreading out documents and papers, but it also supplies the means whereby they can be kept safely locked up. By manipulating an ingenious mechanism, the semicircular, slatted shutter can be rolled away round a cylindrical bar hidden inside the body of the desk. This invention was all the rage during the next period and *ébénistes* like Teuné specialised in *bureaux à cylindre* (see Glossary).

Round about 1770–5, furniture reflects the triumph of the return to antiquity. As always, some makers are still behind their times, especially in the provinces, but the characteristics of the new style have now become firmly established.

2 | The Techniques

▶ *Wood*

Veneering and marquetry techniques had reached such a fantastic degree of perfection that it was impossible to make any further advance in this field.

We should, however, take note that large areas of mahogany are gradually becoming more frequent. Here the *ébéniste* achieves a new effect by exploiting the intrinsic beauty of the wood grain. He uses roe, strongly dotted, twisted and curly-grained mahogany (see Plate xxvi). Mahogany now has a new function: for the first time we find solid mahogany seat furniture. Georges Jacob was probably the master mind behind this innovation. Thus we begin to see the breakdown of that rigorous distinction by which the *menuisiers*, who used native trees for solid carved furniture, were segregated from the *ébénistes*, who used exotic woods for veneering and marquetry. Satinwood, hardly used at all under Louis XV, is employed much more often, and ebony swings back into fashion.

Although veneers and bold geometrical marquetry patterns (thin fillets framing lozenges, rectangles, etc.) do tend to dominate the scene, especially after 1785, brilliantly coloured floral marquetry is nevertheless still very popular. Some of the *ébénistes* like Riesener stay loyal to their old flower motifs right up to the Revolution. Bouquets of flowers tied by ribbon-knots, or pastoral trophies, still form central motifs on the drop-front of a secretaire or the façade of a commode. These marquetry designs in the centre of panels are often arranged in the shape of an oval medallion suspended from a bow of ribbon; the rest of the panel may be filled in by a plain veneer or geometrical marquetry.

▶ *Porcelain and Lacquer*

The search for an ever-richer polychromy led *ébénistes* to insert plaques of porcelain in the panels of their furniture. The white backgrounds of Sèvres plaques, for instance, are painted with garlands or sprigs of flowers, bouquets, attributes of the rustic or pastoral life – even animals. Round, square or rectangular, they make a pretty ornament on the drop-front of a secretaire, a plaque at the junction of two cross-stretchers or on the bottom shelf of a table, or yet again the main panel of a *jardinière* (plant-stand). We even find curved plaque adorning the friezes of small round tables (see Plate xxvii). Sometimes a Wedgwood plaque may be used instead of one from Sèvres. The English ceramist's favourite motifs were minute, extremely delicate figures, copied from ancient classic

xxv *Drop-front Secretaire*

cameos and moulded in low white relief on a pale blue background. Oriental lacquers and French varnishes continue to be used as in the previous period.

▶ *Metals (japanned tin, iron, steel, brass, bronze)*

A few metals begin to appear on furniture, though in a strictly limited fashion. Plaques of kiln-fired japanned tin serve to decorate some of the furniture and the *jardinières*; they are also inlaid in the tops of certain small tables. Usually they are painted with flowers (see Glossary).

Gilt wrought-iron appears in the form of table legs copied from the ancient relics unearthed at Herculaneum and Pompeii. Metal objects were the only ones which had managed to survive prolonged burial under the ashes; it was therefore considered a good idea to imitate them by using the same kind of materials. This explains why *athéniennes* (perfume burners) had metal supports.

Steel begins to be used in decoration: plaques of burnished steel serve as a base for gilt bronze mounts; plaques of finely incised steel (see Plates xx and xxi) also decorate the friezes of furniture.

Brass is employed much more often. It is used in long narrow strips to outline the general contour of a piece or to frame the panels (see Plate xxiii). Pierced galleries, also in brass, surround the flat tops of desks (see Plate xx) or tables (see Plate xxvii). The more modest Louis XVI furniture was reduced to this as its sole form of ornament. Lastly, narrow brass fillets are inlaid into the grooves of flutes and brass rings encircle pilasters. Leleu was probably responsible for launching this technique.

Bronze mounts show a much higher standard of craftsmanship on the whole than they did in the previous period. *Ébénistes* compensate for severity of structural form and monotony of unbroken veneered surfaces with sumptuous bronze accessories (see Plates xxi and xxvi). Bronze mounts are usually confined to friezes, casings (sometimes in the shape of a lion's paw), handles and keyhole plates. Frieze decoration is taken from classical antiquity (flutes, triglyphs, guttae, etc.) and is always chased with the utmost delicacy.

The motifs are usually very small and repetitive. We find an assortment of *raies de cœurs* (see Fig. 13), imbricated scale-work (see Fig. 16), egg-and-dart moulding, pearl beading and Greek-keys (see Fig. 15 and Plate XIX), etc.

Even so, antiquity is not the bronze-worker's only source of inspiration. The art of the *tapissier* exerted a considerable influence on Louis XVI furniture decoration: mock draperies, ribbon streamers, festoons, twisted cords, tassels and fringes are unexpected challengers to the supremacy of standard classic ornament.

Handles are still of the drop type, either simple rectangles or rings enclosing a circular motif (see Plate XX). Some fixed handles are still to be seen, in the form of garlands held by ribbon-knots or hooks made to look like lion's masks.

The most celebrated bronze-worker of the day is Pierre Gouthière (see Plate XXII). His rendering of floral decoration is unparalleled for its technical perfection, but in spite of this the tremendous wealth of detail on which he bestowed a masterly ease, loving care and superb elegance, sometimes gives an over-rich and overcharged appearance to his work. This highly skilled *ciseleur* also made some innovations in gilding technique: hitherto it had been done by the gold-leaf or mercury process – he introduced a matt finish (see Chap I, p. 40).

3 | Decoration and Structure

Within a space of ten years, from 1760–5 to 1770–5, decoration had been completely revolutionised. The 'return to antiquity' made Greek and Roman motifs compulsory. Most of the pattern-books from which artists of this period drew their inspiration do not differentiate between Greek or Roman art. There is no definite criterion guiding the choice of borrowed motifs. The models are taken from the widest possible range of ancient monuments, even those which bear no resemblance to each other whatsoever; date and style are of small importance. We might for instance find the discreet ornamental carving of a fifth-century Greek temple reproduced on the very same sheet of diagrams as the heavily encrusted decoration of a Roman triumphal arch at the time of the decline. The radical difference between the pure good taste of the one, stripped of all unnecessary detail, and the ponderous, overbearing majesty of the other, has been missed altogether.

Yet there is nothing servile about such imitation; these artists show a sure, discerning eye, a refinement of taste and a sound appraisal of what was needed in French art at that time; they have the wit therefore not to make indiscriminate or slavish imitations of the decorative motifs previously used by artists of the Renaissance or the *grand siècle*.

Devotees of the new style are looking for one thing above all from ancient art – an example of clarity and simplicity: for this reason they turn time and again to the Greeks rather than to the Romans. They depend on the undisputed authority of ancient art to win their struggle against the complexity and confusion of Rococo, but the eventual reinstatement of calm, steady line and sober ornament, springs from a fundamentally new attitude of mind, not from a servile imitation.

As a result, although Louis XVI furniture is based on classical forms, it still retains the grace and fantasy of the previous period. Artists accustomed to acknowledge no master save their own inspiration can hardly be expected to submit to the yoke of a foreign art overnight.

Certainly it is true that after 1760 furniture decoration is flooded with columns, pilasters, dentils, triglyphs, guttae, flutes (see Plate xxi), Greek-keys (see Plate xix), wave-bands, interlaced patterns, imbricated scalework, *raies de coeur*, rosettes, egg-and-dart motifs, pearl beading, lions' masks and paws (see Plate xxvi) etc., but these elements are treated on a small scale and executed with great finesse almost as if they were pieces of jewellery – the bronze mounts are an example of this. They stay discreetly in their place and do not overburden the piece. At the same time there is also a trend, one which we might perhaps call 'naturalistic', that serves to counteract the austerity of classical motifs. Late eighteenth-century philosophers, notably Rousseau and Bernardin de Saint-Pierre, preached a return to the rustic life. Decorative art is quick to follow this latest fashion and leaves, flowers, fruit, pastoral attributes, musical instruments, etc., mingle harmoniously with classical motifs on a great deal of this furniture, softening the severe formality of Greek and Roman decoration.

We might also mention Marie-Antoinette's influence here: the *ébénistes de la Couronne* compiled with the queen's personal taste by scattering their decorative designs with flowers, roses in particular, which they treated in a realistic and charmingly delicate fashion.

The *tapissier*'s influence is also responsible for the appearance of pleasantly frivolous motifs, quite out of keeping with the austerity of classical art. Ribbon-knots are the commonest of these motifs, but we also see a number of draperies, fringes and festoons that make a welcome and charming decoration for uncompromisingly naked or austere friezes; ring drawer-handles are made in the form of twisted cords (see Plate xvii) and the bundles of arrows which often form table- or seat-legs ('quiver' legs) are bound with ribbons.

All these decorative themes obey the venerable rules of the strictest possible symmetry. We could even go so far as to say that the Louis XVI style carries this principle of balance in decoration to the extreme. One of the most invariable and characteristic rules of Louis XVI ornament is the repetition of small motifs along one line – pearl beading, *piastres*, Greek-keys, interlaced patterns, *raies de coeur*, Vitruvian scrolls, etc.

Structure becomes architectural: great emphasis is placed on correct proportion, increased dimensions and the balance of one mass against another. Graceful curves are gradually left behind as the century progresses and furniture structure becomes more geometrical. This is the triumph of straight lines, sharp edges, and smooth unbroken surfaces. Such uncompromising rigidity is satisfying to one's reason: the right-angled joints give maximum strength, they are often masked by a cubical wooden block and the different parts of the piece of furniture are clearly defined. The decoration leaves the basic structural form as it is, in all its austerity: narrow bands (see Plate xxiii) or galleries of brass (see Plate xx) accentuate the form but make no attempt to soften it. Panels are usually square, rectangular or trapezoid.

Their shape is nearly always accentuated by bronze accessories (pearl beading or dentils), or by one or more fillets of wood in a colour that contrasts strongly with the panel as a whole.

According to their individual inclinations, *ébénistes* adopted these new forms more or less exactly. Paul Avril for one tends to be somewhat uncompromisingly severe, Fernand Schwerdfeger to be heavily architectural (see Plate xxvi), and Adam Weisweiler a little over-precise though exquisitely refined and elegant (see Plate xxi); but alongside these there are other *ébénistes* better able to adapt their talents and thus avoid such extreme austerity – the inevitable outcome of principles beloved by the ancients. These *ébénistes* know how to temper the exigencies of the 'Greek' style: furniture legs remain slightly bowed; the corners of square or rectangular panels are scooped out and rosettes are set in the empty spaces; the oblique sides of a trapeze are made concave (Riesener) and here and there a band of floral scrollwork twists itself round a straight line; an enchanting, dainty bronze motif sets off an otherwise unbroken surface of veneer, or a vigorous moulding perhaps accentuates the contour of a back or a seat rail.

Little evidence of the ancient work had so far come to light, but the fact that artists of taste interpreted it freely meant that the Louis XVI period was spared the mistakes made in the Napoleonic period. Louis XVI furniture is certainly modelled on a foreign art, but it manages to retain a charming and decidely French originality.

4 | The Different Types of Furniture

▶ *Seat Furniture*

There are as many different kinds of seats as there were in the preceding period and their shapes are even more varied. Broadly speaking, straight lines predominate and the different sections of the seat are simultaneously defined and held together by clear-cut right-angled joints.

The arm-chair back is still often *cabriolet*, but straight backs gradually become the order of the day. Some backs are simple squares or rectangles, but this severe contour can be modified by making the top rail of the square or rectangle dip downwards in a graceful curve. Other backs are *en chapeau* (alternative names: *en hotte* or *en anse de panier* – 'in the shape of a basket handle') or medallion-shaped; the latter is typical of the Louis XVI period (see Plate XVIII). Seats are square, circular, trapezoid, or straight at the back and sides, and very slightly bowed in front. The seat rail may be decorated with *piastres, raies de coeurs* or pearl beading, or yet again it may have a straight moulding decorated by a simple ribbon-knot in the centre. The arms are invariably fitted with arm-pads; they are joined to the back-rest in a more or less exaggerated curve. The scrolled arm supports are seldom set back on the side rails now; they are a direct continuation of the legs, but are incurvate so that ladies may sit down comfortably in their still fashionable panniered skirts. Legs are vertical, '*à l'antique*'. The most popular form is the 'quiver' leg ('*en carquois*'), in other words a tapering column fluted vertically or spirally. The feathered ends of the arrows – which justify this leg's name – are not always shown. The flutes are sometimes cabled, ie. each groove is filled up to a certain height by a narrow convex moulding. Some of the more complicated legs are made to resemble a bundle of arrows or spears cross-bound with ribbons; the arrow feathers or iron spear-heads provide a decoration at either end of the leg. The leg is joined at right angles to the seat rail, and is headed by a square block called a *dé de raccordement*, carved on its two visible faces with a rosette (see Plate XVIII), marguerite, or some circular motif. We find the same features repeated on the *fauteuils de bureau, fauteuils en confessional, bergères, marquises, duchesses, canapés,* etc.

Louis XVI chairs (i.e. those without arms) deserve special attention. Although their legs and seats are in every way similar to those on arm-chairs, their backs show many more elegant refinements. Of course we still have solid backs – square, rectangular or medallioned – which are not very different from arm-chairs, but we also have some very light, elegant chairs with pierced backs. The lyre motif is most fashionable (see Plate XVIII); we also find backs in the shape of a wheatsheaf or a wicker-work basket, or backs made to look like an arcade by means of a row of tapering or fluted colonnettes. The *menuisiers* allow their imagination free rein and one example of this (used as the central motif for some chair-backs) is the *montgolfière* or balloon shape, extremely popular in all decorative art round about 1785 (see Glossary).

Most seats are either painted or gilt. We still find some where the wood is left in its natural state but at the beginning of the century polychrome painting comes into fashion. We are not in a position to give a definitive opinion on this subject, because the great majority of seats we have inherited have been scraped down, regilt and repainted, but it appears that towards the end of the century artists were inclined to avoid strong polychrome effects and concentrate on pale colours such as white or lilac. Beds are still made in the French or Polish style.

▶ *General Furniture*

Solid wood Louis XVI *armoires* are rare; generally they are the product of provincial workshops and keep the curved Louis XV contours. Only a few ornamental motifs – flutes, pearl beading, etc. – betray the fact that they were made at a later date.

The *vitrine* (glass cabinet) is an interesting Louis XVI creation. This is a small cupboard or *bas d'armoire* (see Glossary), generally with a very restrained decoration and glass panes instead of solid doors.

The *bibliothèque* (book-case) is also a derivation of the *armoire* and a close cousin of the *vitrine*. Until about 1770, simple wall cupboards were fitted into the panelling for lack of any proper book-cabinet. The commonest form of *bibliothèque* is made in two sections: the lower one is closed in by two solid wooden doors, and the upper one either by glass panes or brass wire trellis-work panels.

All the countless little tables so fashionable under Louis XV continue to be made. They simply assume straight lines and a classical decoration.

We should, however, make a special point of mentioning dining-tables which make their appearance here. They are an imitation of the English dining-table, usually extending, and are round or oval, manufactured by the *ébénistes* and not the *menuisier*.

The *bouillotte* table is another Louis XVI innovation. Designed exclusively for the game of *bouillotte*, it is round with a marble top surrounded by a low brass gallery; it has four 'quiver' legs and its frieze contains two small drawers and two pull-out flaps.

The *jardinière* or, to be more precise, *table à fleurs* was a by-product of the 'nature' cult inspired by philosophers like Rousseau. It is made on the general lines of a rectangular box standing on four legs, and is often decorated with japanned tin panels or Sèvres china plaques.

The *chiffonnière* undergoes a marked transformation; it becomes solely round or rectangular. The *tricoteuse* is the same as a *chiffonnière* except that its top is surrounded by a high rim intended to prevent balls of wool from rolling off. The rim may either be in solid wood or gilt wire trellis-work.

The *athénienne* is an ingenious little object in the form of a tripod composed of three wooden console legs, carved and gilt, supporting a bowl-shaped brass perfume-burner, coloured a mock ancient bronze. These wooden legs are frequently substituted by metal ones (green patinated bronze, tin, iron, steel) in an attempt to make a close imitation of furniture dug up from Herculaneum and Pompeii. *Athéniennes* were put to many different uses and we may pick out no less than eight from an advertisement in a newspaper of the day; we might mention those of a small console table, plant stand, chafing dish, work table, *vide-poche* (see Glossary) – even a goldfish bowl.

The vogue for mechanical furniture gave rise to the *table à la Tronchin*; in fact this kind of convertible bedside-cum-toilet table was first invented in 1777 by the *ébéniste* Louis Dufour. It was not until a few years later that it was nicknamed *Tronchin*, after a somewhat quackish doctor (see Glossary). It has a double top and stands on four straight legs. The upper section of the top may be raised and adjusted to any height by means of a small handle controlling four ratchets hidden in the table-legs.

As was the case under Louis XV, *ébénistes* continued to

XXVI *Console Table, Louis XVI*

multiply their shapes *ad lib.*, and apart from those types of table already described above, there were *tables itinérantes* (occasional tables), marble-topped tea-tables, *guéridon* tables, known as *serviteurs fidéles,* comprising three circular shelves, each slightly smaller than the next centred at intervals round a slender shaft, and others (see Glossary).

▶ *Bureaux*

The Louis XV *bureau plat* still continues to exist, but the newly invented *bureau à cylindre* (see Glossary) tends to gain precedence. Two modifications have now been made to its prototype – the *bureau du Roi*. The first concerns the closing device : the shutter is no longer made of narrow linked slats ; these have been replaced by a rigid semicircular shutter. The second modification concerns the legs ; the *bureau du Roi* stood on four tall legs, but the Louis XVI *bureau à cylindre* sometimes has a set of drawers going right down to the ground on either side of the writer. François Teuné, the *ébéniste*, specialised in this type of desk.

This principle 'gives birth' so to speak to the *bureau ministre* which is none other than a *bureau plat* with the optional addition of its *cartonnier* (paper rack), and with drawers fitted on either side of the writer. Another version is the *bureau à gradin* (see Plate xx). This kind of desk with eight legs had already become popular in the seventeenth century.

The first examples of the *secrétaire à abattant vertical* (vertical drop-front secretaire), also known as a *secrétaire en armoire,* date back to about 1740. They do not, however, come into general use until the Louis XVI period. Although they are divided into two sections, top and bottom, the carcase is made in one piece and is the same size and shape as a small *armoire.* The lower section comprises a cupboard compartment closed in by solid or sliding doors (see Plate xix). These doors sometimes conceal a set of drawers ; at other times the drawers may be open to view. The upper section is opened by means of a drop-front which serves as a small writing-table when lowered. The inside is fitted with various receptacles (pigeon-holes, drawers, recesses) to take ink, paper, pens, documents, etc. Occasionally space may be

xxvii *Work Table, Louis XVI*

found for a shallow drawer running the full length of the piece to be inserted between the cornice and the top of the drop-front. This massive, architectural piece of furniture with canted corners, cornice and cymatium is perfectly in keeping with the principles underlying an ancient classic revival.

One charming, albeit transient, creation of the Louis XVI style is the *bonheur-du-jour* (see Glossary). This is a small-sized (often a lady's) desk composed of a table with a miniature low cabinet fixed to the rear edge of the top, containing shelves for books and papers. This small cabinet may be made in many different forms: it can be a simple shelf closed in by one or more doors in solid wood or glass; it can also be a set of drawers open to view or concealed, either by doors or a slatted sliding shutter. Some *bonheurs-du-jour* have a lower shelf joining the legs, decorated with marble slabs, surrounded by a brass gallery and slightly recessed in front (see Plate XXI) so that the writer may sit with her legs in a more comfortable position. The very name of these small articles, which were always made to a high standard of craftsmanship, is a fair indication of their immense popularity.

▶ *Commodes, Corner Cupboards, Console Tables*

The numerous commodes manufactured in the Louis XVI period may be classified under two general types. The first is the commode with three drawers resting on short claw, peg-top, or pedestal, etc., feet. These three principal drawers are sometimes surmounted by a shallow drawer, or three in a row. The second has only two drawers. Those commodes with longer, much lighter and more elegant legs retain their Louis XV shape for a long time: a more or less exaggerated *pied-de-biche*. In addition to this they often have a central projection or break-front, which tends to divide the piece up vertically into three sections. In the same way as with tables, the Louis XVI *ébénistes* made great efforts to revive the traditional shapes of commodes: they created a succession of different pieces, all deriving from the commode and intended for many and varied purposes.

The *commode à vantaux* is probably another version of the *encoignure* and has either two or three doors concealing shelves

or drawers as the case may be. The semicircular commode –
known as a *demi-lune* nowadays – generally has two drawers in
front and two curved doors on the sides. In the type of commode *à coins arrondis*, the middle part is rectilinear and closed
in by doors, whilst the sides are made into tiers of open
shelves. These small shelves often have marble tops and are
surrounded by a brass gallery. The side panels lining the
inside of each shelf are sometimes fitted with mirrors. It is a
mistake to call this piece of furniture a *desserte*. It seems tha
the mirrors were intended to enhance the beauty of any
delicate little ornaments that might be placed there. There
are two gorgeous examples of these commodes in the Louvre,
made by Beneman and decorated with bronze fittings chased
by Gouthière, each bearing Marie-Antoinette's cipher.

The *encoignure* accompanies and complements the commode;
it has the same features; either it is closed in by a door or it
remains open with a shallow drawer inserted below the top.
The shelves may also have marble tops and be framed by a
pierced brass gallery.

The *console à pied-de-biche* disappears almost completely.
However, there are some curious surviving examples, such as
the console made by the *menuisier* Chollot, to a highly complex
design, where we can see a mixture of Louis XV and Louis
XVI elements. The typical Louis XVI console has straight
legs and is rectangular, trapezoid (see Plate XXVI), or
semicircular. Its frieze may contain one or perhaps two very
shallow drawers; it may also have a back panel, but this is
very rare.

The Louis XVI *ébénistes*, therefore, did not compare un-
favourably with their predecessors. They created just as
many and just as original new pieces at the end of the century
as were created in the Louis XV period. The outstanding
qualities of this furniture are a distinctly French harmony and
elegance; this is because their imitation of ancient art is far
from being literal, and the whole object of the artisan's
efforts is to create furniture that will be perfectly adapted to
the needs of a society which is both sophisticated and entirely
devoted to its material comforts.

CHAPTER EIGHT

DIRECTORY AND EMPIRE |

1 | The Formation of the Empire Style: Directory Period

The brief period which separated the Louis XVI from the Empire style was given the arbitrary name of Revolutionary or Directory period. We might say, in defence of the latter name, that the experiments tried out over a period of about ten years with the aim of modifying decorative art in general and modernising the 'Greek' style in particular, culminated only under the Directory: it was not until approximately 1797 that the new forms advocated by the *avant-garde* designers and *ébénistes* were generally adopted for everyday household furniture. It was certainly no easy matter to create a properly coherent style under social and economic conditions as violently upset as they were in this period. In effect, the *Directoire* style extends over three different political régimes: the Revolutionary government (1789–95), the Directory (1795–9) and the Consulate (1799–1804). We are therefore faced with a series of phases, rather than one style with consistent and well-defined characteristics. One fact alone is certain; in 1789 furniture was still made in the pure Louis XVI style; in 1804 it was made in the Empire style.

How were artisans led to renew the aesthetics of their furniture, and under what influences?

There are several conflicting trends at this time; *ébénistes* of the old régime react differently according to their several temperaments. Some of them refuse to modify their style; they go on working for the Crown right until the very last moment; once their chief client disappears from the scene they only carry on their work in order to earn their living and take no further interest in artistic research (Saunier, Riesener). Others give up work before the Directors have even come to power (Wolf, Roger Van der Cruse La Croix), and those still left who are more far-sighted and adaptable start working in the latest fashion (Beneman, Lelarge, Nadal) purely to make money; these men are not true innovators; they cannot claim to have evolved the new style. The real creative spirits are the very young *ébénistes* who had not worked under the old régime, or at least had acquired their masterships only a few years before the Revolution (Gruber, Lehaene). Still more effective leaders of the new style are those designers, painters and architects who have been fired with enthusiasm for the new archaeological finds; Georges Jacob, the best *ébéniste* of the period, is in many cases merely an executant. The bold, forward-looking work he had produced under the old régime naturally marks him out as the enthusiastic right-hand man for the new team of artists.

The first symptoms of the *Directoire* style can be traced back to the latter years of Louis XVI's reign. The *Bibliothèque Nationale* still has the painted and measured sketches of an Etruscan-style piece conceived in 1786 by the architect Le Queu for the *Hôtel Montholon*. As early as 1789 David placed orders with Georges Jacob for a suite of 'Etruscan' pieces to furnish his studios in the Louvre. The *ébéniste* contracted to execute sketches by David and his pupil Charles Moreau. This furniture included bronze curule chairs, with the ends of each member made in the shape of animal heads or feet; there were some dark mahogany chairs too, with red wool cushioned seats and decorated with black palmettes. The *maître* used these chairs in some of his paintings.

Round about 1790 the designer Jean-Demosthène Dugourc also emerges as one claiming to be the inventor of the new style. Having enlisted the *ébéniste* Grognard's help, he produced a number of 'Etruscan' models for the use of Mme. Elisabeth and the Comte d'Artois. On the whole, these designs are not nearly so heavily ostentatious as those by

David. Here we find practically all the 'Etruscan' innovations, intermingled with pure 'Greek' decorative motifs; seat-legs are in the form of cornucopiae or extremely slender spindles, tapering to a point; arm-supports represent female terminal busts or winged spirits, alternatively they terminate in animal heads; backs are rolled over or half-moon shaped. On the other hand there is nothing Etruscan about the proposed colour scheme for the upholstery – light, gay colours in the Louis XVI tradition. These attempts at innovation, however, are the product of a minority of artists and have no effective influence on furniture as a whole for several years to come. In most interiors, furniture is still built on Louis XVI lines. Its appearance is kept up to date by means of a few ornamental details. Financial stringency had resulted in the suppression of veneers, marquetry designs and bronze mounts. Instead, this furniture is in solid wood, generally beech. It is painted in light colours and its decoration is reduced to the occasional very thin fillet (green, blue, gold, etc.) which breaks up a monotonous panel or frames a central motif. Mahogany veneers or solid carved mahogany are only used for luxury pieces. This dense, close-grained wood is perfectly suited to austere imitations of classical art.

The furniture trade undergoes radical changes at this time. When the guilds are abolished, official identification stamps are suppressed: it becomes difficult to trace each *ébéniste*'s work; only a few families like the Jacobs or the Lemarchands stick faithfully to the old tradition. Veneering and marquetry-work disappear almost completely, *ébénistes* properly speaking cease to exist. Furniture artisans are free to adopt either technique as they choose; most pieces are in solid wood, but if the occasion arises, a *menuisier* will veneer his furniture. He also reverts to the practice of inlay-work, either in a different kind of wood from the carcase (ebony, satinwood), or mother-of-pearl, brass or pewter. The vogue for pewter was very transitory; it was abandoned after 1800. Finally, the creative role of the furniture-maker gradually diminishes. In a great many cases, the artisan is simply obliged to make a faithful reproduction of a detailed design. The unfortunate consequences of this practice are not yet evident under the Directory, since although Georges Jacob might sometimes execute a piece designed by David, or Jacob Desmalter one designed by Berthault for Mme. Récamier, both these men are skilled designers in their own right: of their own free will they make an exception to their normal practice by translating another artist's idea in terms of wood. Yet it will not be long before artisans come to believe the epitome of art to be a faithful, slavish copy of any given model.

The transition from the Louis XVI to the Empire style may therefore be said to take place in two stages. Up to about 1795–7, almost all the modifications apply to decoration. After 1797, when economic and social conditions improve, a wider public is able to take advantage of the innovations which until then had been reserved for a small group of artists. Then the structural form of furniture follows suit.

It cannot be emphasised too strongly that this sequence of changes is valid only for Paris. In the provinces, furniture continues to be made in the Louis XVI style.

▶ *Decoration*

Some decorative motifs were the direct consequence of short-lived fashions inspired by political or military events, nevertheless a number of motifs handed down from the Louis XVI period were still perpetuated. The palmette is one of these. We may note its appearance round about 1785; it holds its ground all through the Directory (see Plate xxiv) and crops up again under the Empire. It is widely used under the Directory; we see it repeated on bands, friezes or as an applied ornament; it often does duty as a capital.

The lozenge, like the palmette, has already been used in the previous period, but under Louis XVI it had been merely one of the many elements that went to make up the geometrical marquetry decoration. Under the Directory it is constantly used on its own. It may well form the sole decorative feature on a solid wood panel; a dark wood like mahogany might also be inlaid with a thin lozenge-shaped fillet of lighter wood – satinwood for example. Lozenges are simply painted in on the more modest pieces (black on brick red, green or gold on white). These painted or inlaid lozenges may be used to frame central motifs: for example scenes copied from Greek vases. Another extremely common use of the lozenge is to decorate the small square blocks on the corners of seat rails.

After the Revolution a whole host of large geometrical figures fulfil the same purpose as lozenges: such as hexagons, regular or oblong octagons, and ellipses drawn out to varying lengths.

A number of realistic and fanciful animals are favourite motifs of this new style. The swan enjoyed a vogue that lasted through the Empire without any signs of dying out: we already find it used for arm-supports, bed uprights (Mme. Récamier's bed painted by Berthault), wash-bowl stands and still more often as an applied bronze ornament. The griffon embarks modestly on its career, biding its time before making a bid for supremacy under the Empire. The serpent is granted a few favours. Two serpents, each with a ball between its teeth, extend from the seat- to the top-rail of a chair designed by Dugourc in 1790. The male sphinx comes into fashion after the Egyptian campaign; it takes the place of the female-busted Greek sphinx employed in the Louis XVI period. By a curious hybridisation, the Greek female sphinx sometimes wears a *klaft*, the Egyptian royal head-dress.

Lastly, certain special motifs are adopted for a brief period; their appearance and disappearance are directly connected with political events. After 1789 Revolutionary emblems are hastily plastered over furniture that is structurally pure Louis XVI. We also see 'Storming of the Bastille' scenes, clasped hands (the symbol of fraternity), triangles with an eye in the middle, (the symbol of clairvoyance), Phrygian bonnets, trees of liberty, pikes, lances, etc. Imagination runs wild. No extravagance is spared on furniture design. Thus we find that before he left for Italy in 1796 the young General Bonaparte ordered a suite of 'patriotic' furniture from Jacob Desmalter for his mansion in the Rue Chantereine. The bed incorporates a bell canopy painted in the colours of the French national flag: the eight stools are made like drums with cords stretched over them but yellow hide has been substituted for the parchment tops to make them practicable as seats.

XXVIII *Cabinet, Louis XVI*

A few years later, in about 1798, the Egyptian campaign brings sphinxes, scarabs, lotus flowers (see Plate xxiv), caryatids, and pyramids into fashion. However, from 1799 onwards when Napoleon starts fancying himself as a modern Caesar, furniture decoration is invaded by a crowd of martial attributes: trophies of arms, panoplies, bundles of spears, helmets, crossed Roman swords, lictors' fasces, etc.

At the very end of the period under discussion we find the emergence of symbolic figures: under the Empire artists really let themselves go on this type of ornament. Under the Directory we can already see winged genii, figures symbolising fame (nymphs holding palms or crowns) or fortune (elegant female figures, like those designed by Berthault for Mme Récamier, standing on a terrestrial globe).

▶ *Structure*

The need for clarity and simplicity meant that all complicated shapes and unnecessary articles of furniture were abolished. There is a growing trend towards geometrical form, straight lines, simple curves. Ornament never disguises the structural form; it is always discreet and sometimes lacking altogether.

In all honesty we cannot credit this period with any new creations, but, out of a strange desire for change and novelty, furniture dealers and contemporary periodicals – the *Journal des Dames et des Modes* for instance, published by La Mésangère from 1797 to 1802, to mention just one of the better known ones – took a fiendish delight in changing the terminology adopted under Louis XVI. Thus a small commode comes to be called a *chiffonnière*, and *athénienne* a *vide-poche*, a *bonheur-du-jour* a *table à gradins*, etc. To the uninitiated this might indicate novelty, but in fact all there is is copied purely and simply from the shapes previously fashionable under Louis XVI.

The different types of furniture gradually decrease in number. A great variety of commodes had been created in the Louis XVI period. The *Directoire* style does not, however, profit by the previous period's lessons, and nearly all commodes revert to a single standard model: this is a commode with short legs, frequently in the form of lions' paws, and containing three drawers. *Bureaux* are often made with drop-fronts. Tables, though, are more varied: we have circular dining-tables, *tricoteuses*, bedside tables, shaving tables, *jardinières* and *guéridons*. Each of these is well proportioned, with smooth surfaces and sharp corners. Commodes and *secrétaires* are decorated with terminal figures, columns or unfluted pilasters. Chimeras, swans, sphinxes, griffons, etc., are used for table-legs.

As always, seat furniture is the living expression of the society that uses them. Such pieces change more rapidly and more markedly than other types of furniture.

Seat-legs are frequently square in section, the rear legs being curved backwards in the form of a sabre: this is called the 'Etruscan' leg (see Plate xxiv). In some rare cases the front legs follow the same curve, but more often they are a tapering spindle (see Plate xxiv), turned and ringed, or straight and square in section, or yet again baluster-shaped (see Plate xxiv). X-shaped legs were inspired by the Roman curule chair. The X is slightly curved and terminates in lions' paws. A baluster traverse joins the two X's to make the seat firm. The X might also feature two cornucopiae with the points resting on the ground. Alternatively, the decoration on the X might be given over to serpents. Arm-rests very often terminate in rams', eagles', leopards' or lions' heads. In these cases the arm-supports are in the form of colonnettes or balusters, but in a great many instances the arm-rests provide evidence of some very advanced research: female busts, winged genii, swans, sphinxes and griffons may feature just as often on arm-rests as on legs. As early as the Egyptian campaign (1798) arm-supports are made as prolongations of the front feet without a break at the seat rail; this was adopted almost as a standard formula under the Empire.

Backs show an astonishing variety: solid padded backs are the exception, pierced backs the more general rule. For instance a broad traverse, flat or half-moon shaped, and fixed level with the back of a seated person, may be supported either by two uprights continuing the rear legs or by a more elaborately worked decorative motif. This type of back appears as early as 1786 in the design submitted by Le

Queu for furniture in the *Hôtel Montholon*; David also uses it for seats in the *Assemblée Nationale*. Decoration on the traverse may be carved, inlaid or painted, but it can also appear on a strip of silk or painted paper (see Plate xxiv) stretched over the wood. Popular motifs range from a simple lozenge to a scene copied from a Greek vase. Later on we see backs with the upper traverse scrolled over. The traverse usually has a very restrained decoration, but what makes these backs so elegant and interesting is the pierced motifs linking the traverse to the seat. Pierced backs are nothing new – they existed in the Louis XVI period – but under the Directory this part of the seat becomes much more original in its decoration. The plainer backs are formed by a simple cross-piece, a square lozenge, pierced lattice-work cut from a single piece of mahogany, a network of cords held apart by discs, a single large palmette, several palmettes, or a geo-metrical design of palmettes. Yet more ambitious devices are not hard to come by: here and there we may find a lyre, an hour-glass silhouette, a tripod, an amphora, a triangle with an eye in the middle, a war trophy, two seated confronted sphinxes, etc. Two innovations destined for great success during the next century make their first appearance under the Directory; a handhold hollowed out of the upper traverse and a turned piece of wood fixed on top of the traverse, so that one can grasp the chair easily.

The more comfortable seats – *bergères, marquises* – that invited one to relax are out of place now. They are all abandoned on the grounds that they are incompatible with the dignity of free citizens, except for the *chaise longue*, now called a *couche à l'antique* or *méridienne*. Nevertheless, one extremely comfortable chair was created under the Directory: the 'gondola' or tub-shaped arm-chair (see Plate xxx). This generally very low chair is a cunning combination of the *fauteuil en cabriolet* and the *fauteuil de bureau*. It has a rounded, all-enveloping back which slopes gently down to meet the seat-rail, thus forming the sides.

There are very few extant pieces by which we may form an opinion on *Directoire* furniture. Nearly all the finest museum pieces are the product of Jacob's enterprise and that of his sons. The general run of contemporary furniture, in native wood, painted and often carelessly put together, has practically all been lost.

Despite some extravagances, due chiefly to two designers, *Directoire* furniture has plenty of grace and charm. Even though it is dominated by classical models and shows a studied severity of form, it has not yet succumbed to the crushing pedantry of the Empire style.

2 | The Empire

The Empire style sprang from a dictator's desire to leave his personal seal on the art of his reign. Napoleon entrusted the task of creating a special decorative art of the Imperial régime to two architects, C. Percier and P.-F.-L. Fontaine. The text which we might well call the 'Empire style manifesto' was not, however, written until 1812 when it served as a preface to a *'Recueil de Décoration Intérieure'* designed by the two artists. The basic principles they set out in this preface are those which govern all artistic creativity from 1804 to 1814. Absolute compliance with the rules of ancient art could hardly be more plainly asserted. 'It would be vain' they say 'to seek for shapes preferable to those handed down to us by the Ancients'. As from 1760, all those concerned either with the theory or practice of art prided themselves on the fact that their work was based solely on these classical shapes. Yet up to the time of the Revolution, artists exercised discretion in their imitation, with the result that French decorative art had retained its native grace and elegance. Under the Directory, however, classical models were copied more stringently, more academically. This phase reaches its climax under the Empire : 'If the study of antiquity should come to be neglected, before long the productions of industry would lose that regulating influence which alone can give the best direction to their ornaments, which in some sort prescribes to every substance the limits within which its claims to please must be confined, which indicates to the artist the best utilisation of forms and fixes their varieties within a circle which they should never overstep'. The prime object therefore is, not to please, but to keep from exceeding the limits prescribed by classical art. Percier and Fontaine, both aware of the inflexibility of such a doctrine, took it upon themselves, theoretically at least, to modify these principles in certain respects. They conceded that works of art had to be adapted to the exigencies of modern life and that it would be foolish to ignore the fact that their contemporaries were technically superior to the ancients. 'The models of antiquity' should 'not be followed blindly but with the discrimination entailed by the manners, customs and materials of the moderns.'

This half-hearted stricture was not heeded in the slightest. Furniture designed by Percier, Fontaine and their imitators retains the artificial, academic character which springs from an over-exact simultaion of a foreign art. The most elementary laws of ease and comfort are sacrificed to frigid archaeology.

A slavish reproduction of ancient art is not the only rule advocated by the two artists. Percier and Fontaine, who were responsible for Imperial art, wanted to make it coherent, homogenous. Lebrun, in Louis XIV's reign, was faced with precisely the same problem. Individual temperament was forced to efface itself before a single conception of art as a whole. 'Furniture is too closely related to interior decoration for an architect to feign indifference to it . . . The basic structure of an edifice is the equivalent of bones in a human body; it should be embellished without being masked completely.' Percier and Fontaine, not content with supplying models for ceilings, panelling, and draperies, designed furniture as well. Through them, the Emperor exerted his own decisive influence. Like most dictators, Napoleon had a taste for pomp and splendour. He wanted his furniture to be on a vast scale and excessively rich. No one could deny that furniture made for the Emperor or his immediate entourage is too big, too heavy and too laden with bronze mounts. Once the 'grand manner' was established it gradually influenced furniture in daily use, even the most commonplace pieces.

The three characteristics, therefore, of Empire furniture are the imitation of ancient art, uniformity, and the trend towards monumental proportions.

3 | The Techniques

▶ *Wood* (*veneering, inlay-work*)

Mahogany was most frequently employed in spite of the difficulties of importation. It came from Santo Domingo, which had just then revolted against France, and various islands held by the British. As early as 1801, in his *Annales du Musée*, Charles Landon opened his campaign in support of native woods: 'We scorn the products of our native soil yet we ourselves possess woods which lack nothing but colour to satisfy the eye. As for hardness and density they are in no way inferior to foreign importations . . .' A few pages later on, Landon gives some very precise formulae for dying native woods. His sensible advice was not really followed up until the Restoration. Although it was a costly process, all *meubles de luxe* under the Empire were made in solid mahogany. Less glamorous pieces were simply veneered. The quality of these veneers is excellent. Artists also reached the stage of veneering wooden seats, table-legs – even round ones – colonnettes decorating commode or secretaire façades etc. The different varieties of mahogany are multiplied indefinitely. There are both light mahoganies and dark mahoganies. Above all there are those mahoganies with a distorted grain, giving an excellent decorative effect (roe, curly-grained, flame-like figures, mottle, striated, etc.). *Ebénistes* begin to use native woods for their more ordinary furniture; but the first half-hearted attempts made in this field under the Empire bear no fruit until after 1815. On account of their similarity to mahogany, first preference goes to the dark woods whose grain forms interesting and decorative patterns. Examples of these are the yew-tree root or strongly dotted thuya wood. The rarer, lighter woods are only used if the grain is attractive enough to merit large panels without further ornamentation. Thus we might find a spotted grain in beech, a watered figure in plane or a flecked pattern in ash, etc. Burr beech, ash and elm begin to be used in quantity. Seats, when not mahogany, are walnut or beech, but still richly painted and gilt.

Inlays of narrow fillets or larger motifs such as laurel and olive crowns, ciphers or rosettes are commonly found. Light woods (satinwood, olive) are set into dark woods (mahogany); alternatively, dark woods (ebony, mahogany, yew) are inlaid into light woods (beech, elm, certain varieties of mahogany). Ivory, mother-of-pearl, brass and even steel inlays are more unusual. They are reserved for high-quality furniture and are never used for anything except ornamental details.

► *Bronze Mounts*

Bronze has an all-important part to play under the Empire. The severe structural forms with large unbroken panel surfaces call for some sort of ornamentation. The bronze mounts used are of exceptionally high quality, wonderfully chased and given a matt gilt finish. Artists like Thomire, Ravrio and Odiot are not above co-operating with the best *ébénistes* of the period, and a great deal of furniture was made whose sole point of interest lay in the bronze mounts (see Plate xxxii). Bronze mounts no longer serve merely to accentuate the structure of a piece, or to protect fragile marquetry with pendants or keyhole plates; they have been entrusted with a much more important mission: that of decorating and giving a personal touch to monotonous uniform mahogany surfaces. Bronze motifs are therefore treated quite differently: they are no longer part of the structure, they now have a value of their own. These are applied bronze ornaments in the true sense of the word, finely chased, independent of each other, constituting their own particular form of decoration and designed on a scale of their own. The subjects they portray are mostly unrelated; we might for instance find on the same secretaire a chariot of Fame, drawn by two chargers, and two confronted lions, each with one paw resting on a bowl. Palmettes, stars, crowns, bees, and interlaced ciphers are frequently strewn haphazard across a frieze, or placed on a colonnette to act as a capital. Although mythological scenes are somewhat stylised, they are gracefully executed. Those large female figures occupying a whole panel are the only ones to offend us by their frequently unappealing stiffness. The same motifs reappear on the clocks and silverware created by contemporary bronze-workers. Thus bronze-work on furniture gradually develops into a specific art, one requiring the skill of specialists.

4 | Decoration and Structure

▶ *Decoration*

Decorative themes under the Empire are seldom new. The *Directoire* style has already brought a number of ancient classical motifs into fashion. Percier and Fontaine, those austere theoreticians, having once accustomed themselves to the majestic ordinance of ancient classical monuments, then disciplined and standardised the various elements of this new ornamental grammar. In the name of reason, proportion and balance, they co-ordinated the incongruous inventions of the preceding period, and, most important of all, they enforced a *more rigorous interpretation* of those motifs which up till then had been treated fancifully and inconsistently. As always happens in the decorative arts, order is synonymous with a lack of imagination.

Attributes of war, already fashionable under the Consulate, reappear: oak, laurel or olive crowns, Roman swords, rapiers, shields, helmets, bows, arrows, quivers. Of the animals, the most popular are swans – featured on Josephine's coat of arms – and the heraldic eagle, symbol of imperial power, but we also find lions, rams, winged or wingless horses and all the mythological animals (sphinxes, dragons, etc.).

Musical instruments also remain in favour. Lyres still do double duty as certain kinds of table-legs or as applied bronze ornaments, but occasionally preference is shown for more typically 'ancient' instruments like sistrums, tubas or rattles.

Room is also found for all manner of geometrical shapes to frame or isolate anecdotal motifs: circles, squares, ovals, lozenges (see Plate xxxii), hexagons, octagons, etc.

Plants and flowers stay the same as in the preceding period: laurels, olive trees, oak trees, palms, water-lilies, trails of ivy, etc.; but all these plants stiffen into over-stylisation. Poppy

xxix *Bed, First Empire*

wreaths or vine leaves are perhaps the only ones to keep a breath of life about them. All the bric-à-brac so dear to the hearts of antique-worshippers continues to be used too: cornucopiae, amphorae, shallow bowls, caducei, tridents, thunderbolts, thyrsi, etc.

The human figure takes refuge in the form of gods and goddesses, nude or robed in classical draperies: figures of Victory holding palms or crowns, sometimes standing on a triumphal car, or Greek dancers with their floating scarves and tunics billowing like sails on a ship. . . . We would hesitate to credit those female terminal busts which all too often adorn furniture uprights with the title of 'human figures'. Crowned royal monograms, stars, bees and an occasional butterfly complete the repertoire.

This very monotonous, impersonal, prosaic decoration usually takes the form of applied bronze ornaments, whose outstanding craftsmanship does much to make up for their lack of originality.

Solid wood-carving disappears except on seat furniture. It stands out in sharp relief and looks very like bronze-work.

▶ *Structure*

The originality of Empire furniture lies much more in its structure than in its decoration. In the eighteenth century furniture had been made to the same scale as man himself, but under the Empire this precept no longer holds good. Furniture dimensions are not in proportion to the human canon; they are determined by the scheme of interior decoration as a whole. Furniture thus becomes an arbitrary creation taking its place in a solemn, grandiose setting. Seats appear as bare, soulless frameworks hung with upholstery materials like beds or windows; they are intended to be seen from the front, lined up against a wall. Upholstery materials therefore assume prime importance. There is none of the personal touch about furniture any longer. It is simply reduced to austere 'heroic' decorative elements, suited to a generation of warriors.

This impersonal, artificial grandeur is obtained chiefly by means of rectilinear forms; wide flat surfaces are broken up

xxx *Gondola Chair, Consulate Period. Arm-chair, First Empire* by right angles. Seats and other furniture confront the eye with undisguised sharp edges. Moulding is banned; not a single chamfer, not a single *doucine* is allowed to soften the angles on this furniture. If a few mouldings should persist, they are so paltry as to have no decorative interest. If an upright still remains in view, it is decorated with a caryatid or a female terminal bust tapering into a quadrangular column. However, uprights are more often hidden beneath a uniform veneer that conceals all joints and evidence of practical construction. The façade may be embellished by colonnettes or animal figures, but these are free-standing in front of the carcase, never engaged. The general structure stays rectilinear and all ornament gives the impression of being superimposed. It is not an integral part of the piece; instead it is treated as an applied decoration with no relation to the basic structural form. The craze for uniform veneered surfaces is so great that even ring handles are left off and key-holes are hardly ever made to attract attention by a bronze motif. Some drawers have no handles at all, being pulled out by the key alone. Keyholes are mere slits cut in the wood, as unobtrusive as possible. We even get to the point where drawers are completely camouflaged by a drop-front. If a bronze handle should still exist as a means for pulling the drawer out, more often than not it is made to look like a patera, a small flat' plate which, from a few feet away, gives the impression of an applied bronze mount. In short, every possible device is used to make furniture appear as a solid uninterrupted block; it has often been said, though this is something of an over-statement, that Empire furniture looked monolithic.

The impression of majesty and power conferred on furniture by its rectilinear form is further heightened by the makers' frequent habit of mounting their furniture on plinths. Beds, and tables in particular, rest on a heavy base. By being raised up in this way, furniture assumes a monumental appearance.

Lastly, that symmetry so beloved by the Ancients applies just as rigorously to overall interior decoration as to the individual items of furniture and their ornamentation. Two identical consoles are often placed either side of a fire-place or a window, in the same way as a pair of *lit bateau* (see below) uprights terminate in two identical scrolls, or as two doors on a *bas d'armoire* (under cupboard) are decorated with two applied bronze figures of Fame, whose tunics fall in exactly similar folds. This deliberately calculated symmetry contributes to the artificial, academic character of Napoleonic furniture.

The rectilinear form and overbearing dimensions of Empire furniture have often been criticised in the name of comfort and intimacy. As early as 1802 Comte P.-L. Roederer raised his voice in protest against the superfluous corners and the horribly sharp edges which require 'a thousand precautions to be taken to avoid being bruised'. We may sum up the situation, however, by saying that most pieces of furniture made between 1804 and 1814 are *meubles d'apparat*, and not suitable for everyday or informal use (see Glossary).

5 | The Different Types of Furniture

The Empire makes no attempt to exploit the ingenious creations of the eighteenth century: certain specialised pieces and seats invented during the eighteenth century fall out of favour completely. Since furniture-makers under the Empire are not concerned with fulfilling the needs of an intimate or luxurious way of life, they retain only the essential items of their eighteenth-century legacy. They reduce seat furniture to two or three main types, renouncing the former infinite variety of small pieces for specific and limited purposes.

▶ *Seats and Beds*

Seats are the first to be affected by this impoverishment. Empire arm-chairs are built on ample proportions; they are not intended to be moved around easily and thus encourage informal conversation, but instead they occupy a more or less permanent position ranged against the wall. Backs are invariably upholstered, rectilinear or rolled-over (see Plate xxx) and occasionally surmounted by a pediment. Seats are square or nearly so. Arm-rests, fitted with pads, have a great variety of supports. In most cases these supports are a continuation of the fore-legs, uninterrupted at the seat-rail; they may be in the form of terminal caryatids, one-legged lions, swans, eagles, chimeras or dragons, all supporting the arm-chair seat from ground level upwards. In other cases where the seat-rail is clearly defined, the arm consoles nearly always feature the same motifs but the rear legs become much more varied. They may be square in section, or, when the seat is in native wood (painted or gilt), they may be carved in bold relief. Alternatively, when the seat is in veneered or solid mahogany, they may be decorated with bronze mounts. Cylindrical, fluted legs compete for favour again with the turned, tapering type. We also come across some legs made up of two superposed balusters. In both these latter examples the rear legs are square in section, sabre-form, curving backwards to a greater or lesser extent. The less formal 'gondola' shape that came into being under the Directory is also very popular.

In addition to arm-chairs and chairs, the Empire made great use of stools. For the same reasons of social precedence that obtained in the *grand siècle*, it was thought suitable to adopt a more democratic kind of seat than the arm-chair, or even the chair. Stools are made in the shape of a double X, linked by a cross-stretcher and given an upholstered top. Arm-chairs, chairs and stools constitute practically the whole range of Empire seats.

There are, however, a few *canapés* – which are simply extra wide arm-chairs – and two sorts of *chaises longues* – with two slightly rolled-over backs – together with that type of *chaise longue* known as a *méridienne* where a third long back links two short backs of unequal height. Beds come in two principal types, but in either case they are meant to be placed in an alcove and seen from the side; this is so much the standard rule that only one of the four faces is given a decoration worthy of interest. Those beds with straight uprights are built on a framework reminiscent of Louis XVI beds, though the latter's slender colonnettes have given way either to thick columns and heavy pilasters, or to mythological animals and classical terminal busts. There are also some beds where the

xxxi *Commode, First Empire*

uprights present an unbroken mahogany surface, lavishly decorated with bronze mounts.

The second type of bed is one of the happiest creations of the Napoleonic period. This is the *lit en gondole*, generally called a *lit bateau* on account of its vague resemblance to a small boat: from the side view we can see two backs of equal height, sloping backwards and rolled-over, linked by a steeply curved traverse that continues the curve of the two backs. There is enough room on the uprights, which are very wide at the base, for the whole ornamental repertoire of the Empire to spread out at will: not only do we find the simple applied bronze palm adapted to fit the curve of the uprights, but dancers, chimeras, cornucopiae and other motifs. There is also another version of the *lit bateau* with one back, built on much lighter lines (see Plate xxix). Both types of bed are often overhung by a canopy made in the same material as that covering the bed. As far as the canopy is concerned, the Empire simply imitates previous fashions.

▶ *Tables*

Large Empire tables are round. The more ordinary ones are simply overlaid with a heavy wooden disc that serves as a top. However, the Empire also makes use of some materials that are unusual in the art of furniture-making: in addition to marble, we find malachite, porphyry, mosaic (*table des maréchaux*, Malmaison), porcelain and glass. These materials may be employed on their own or embedded in wooden friezes and decorated with bronze mounts; alternatively they may form the inlaid decoration on a wood carcase themselves.

The Empire lavishes its greatest originality on the legs of its furniture. Many supports are formed by a single central pillar – column or baluster – standing on a very low plinth. This base is often a curvilinear triangle with concave sides, sometimes fitted with castors. The thick pilasters may sometimes be replaced by mythological animals. All manner of Egyptian, Greek and Roman monsters club together in groups of three and balance table-tops on their heads, shoulders and outspread wings. Designers indulge in a regular orgy of fantasy – the most hybrid and most complex

xxxii *Commode à l'Anglaise, First Empire*

animals that Imperial artists could possibly devise go to make these extraordinary table-supports. Very often *ébénistes* and bronze-workers would collaborate in manufacturing them. Solid mahogany table-legs carved in high, round relief are still to be found, however; also those where metal (iron, gilt or patinated bronze) plays an important or exclusive part.

This style of Empire table looks like an over-magnified *guéridon*. It is so typical of the period that we are apt to forget that some of the shapes created under Louis XVI and the Directory were also repeated under the Empire. These much more varied little tables (square, rectangular and occasionally hexagonal) have nothing new about them except their style of decoration. They introduce a light fantastic note into the cold, oppressively formal *ensembles* created by the architects. Percier on the other hand condemns these little tables, 'like parasitic plants as prolific as they are useless', but we think them utterly delightful precisely because they do not conform to the all-powerful archaeological influence dominating Imperial decorative art.

Work-tables, *tricoteuses*, tea tables, dining-tables, *jardinières*, *tables à coiffer* and shaving tables are so many examples of these ingenious and charming little pieces whose legs are not encumbered by monsters. Lyre- and X-shaped legs at either end of the table-top, slender colonnettes or the standard terminal figures at each corner are commonly employed. One bright new solution to the problem of table-legs consists of a row of uprights joining the frieze to the plinth beneath. This plinth is sometimes solid, but often it is made up of a star having the same number of rays as the table has legs.

We should also devote special attention to the *lavabo* and the *somno*. The Louis XVI *athénienne* now develops into specialised forms. We have already seen that just before the Revolution furniture dealers were advertising its many uses. Under the Empire, the *athénienne* turns into a utility piece. Its three legs, usually in metal, support a shallow bowl and ewer, in other words a wash-basin and water-jug.

The *somno* is a cylindrical bedside table. This solid mahogany piece, shorn of all moulding or even a visible door, is one of those which most deserve to be called monoliths.

Applied bronze ornaments, often representing allegorical divinities, make a vain attempt to brighten up and relieve this heavy and almost totally unattractive piece.

▶ *Psychés (cheval glasses) and Consoles* (see Glossary)

The *psyché* is one of the happiest of Imperial creations. The *Manufacture Royale de Glaces* at Saint-Gobain had hit on a method of producing large-sized mirrors in the early eighteenth century, but it was not until 1768 that mechanical processes made it possible to produce large mirrors in quantity. Furniture design did not really benefit from this innovation until the Empire. The Louis XVI *coiffeuse* sometimes had a small mirror fixed on the inside of one of its lids, but the Empire *table à coiffer* is reduced to a simple rectangular table with lyre- or X-shaped legs. From now on mirrors are made independently. This new item is composed of a heavy base and two uprights with a large mirror suspended in between. In principle, in order to justify its name, the mirror is supposed to be large enough to reflect the full image of a standing person. The base, which is of necessity heavy, comprises a stand formed by mythological animals, or simply by sabre-shaped legs in groups of four or eight; another variation is a solid plinth containing a long drawer. The mirror – round, rectangular, or more often oval – is mounted on a pivot; it can therefore be tilted on its axis between the two columns or pilasters forming the uprights. The uprights are surmounted by various bronze finials – vase, urn, classical head or fir cone – and fitted with branching candelabra at the half-way mark. The empty space between the plinth and the lower curve of the mirror is filled in by a triangular panel with bronze decorations. Other mirrors, made to the same design but much smaller and intended to stand on tables, are wrongly known as *psychés*.

The *consoles d'appliques* (console tables) are also very typical of the Empire period; they are monumental, simple in the extreme and comply easily enough with the demands of symmetry, since it is by no means rare for two matching consoles to be arranged in pairs. The standard form is for a rectangular top to be upheld by four caryatids or by two uprights with applied bronze ornaments. Many consoles have a rear panel, sometimes inlaid with a mirror.

▶ *Commodes, Bureaux, Secretaires*

Of the many new types of commode conceived in the Louis XVI period, only two models survived under the Empire: the commode on short feet containing three drawers (see Plate xxxi) and the commode with two doors concealing drawers or shelves (see Plate xxxii). In the latter case it is more usually called a *bas d'armoire* (under-cupboard) or a *commode à l'anglaise*. Empire innovations in bureaux were very unenterprising. As before, we have *bureaux plats* and *bureaux ministres*. Only their vast proportions, their use of mahogany, their bronze ornaments and complex legs of hybrid animals give these desks an Empire look. A few exceptional pieces have their bases copied from Roman triumphal arches: here three sumptuously decorated 'arches' support a gigantic and massive flat top.

Bureaux à cylindre and *bureaux à abattant* are also commonly found. Only their decoration distinguishes them from those of the Louis XVI period. The *bonheurs-du-jour* which served mostly as ladies' desks in the previous period now become monumental and imposing, losing much of their charm in the process.

The too literal imitation of classical art has thus dulled creative feeling, and although this furniture occasionally reaches the heights of technical perfection, it never possesses that grace and spontaneity which makes eighteenth-century furniture so attractive; it is a true reflection of the aims and ambitions of the warrior generation it was created for: severe and overbearingly formal.

| THE RESTORATION

This title covers a period extending from 1815 to 1850 but, as far as furniture is concerned, we should really distinguish between two successive periods. Under the Bourbons, from 1815 to 1830, furniture design is still dominated by the Napoleonic influence. In spite of many interesting experiments made by top-ranking *ébénistes*, none of them succeeded in establishing a new, properly coherent style.

The crushing influence of the Napoleonic period is mitigated in Louis-Philippe's reign. The *ébénistes'* habit of copying every style from Gothic to Louis XVI, with varying degrees of accuracy, resulted in a collection of hybrid furniture, some of which, however, did turn out successfully. It is under Louis-Philippe that we first see this practice of drawing inspiration from furniture of past generations. *Pastiche* was to enjoy an unheard of popularity under the Second Empire, but the first example of it dates back to approximately 1830.

I | The Restoration under Louis XVIII and Charles X

Restoration furniture is characterised by many different trends. Everything was tried out but no one trend emerged dominant. Until this time the various sovereigns' personal tastes had directed the evolution of art. In fact what had happened was that new ideas were encouraged by orders placed with the royal or imperial *garde-meuble* and the ruling monarch had thus always had a considerable influence, ever since the time of François I.

When Louis XVIII returned to France, he proceeded to settle happily enough in residence, surrounded by his usurper's furniture. It has been said that he even thought highly of his predecessor's innovations. In any case it would have been quite out of the question to make totally new replacements for the *ensembles* that Napoleon had created in the royal palaces: the privy purse was empty. At first alterations were restricted to scratching off the bees and the N's and replacing them by *fleur de lys* and L's. After a few years, however, when the new sovereign was forced by sheer necessity to place some orders, these had to be for furniture that would harmonise with the existing *ensembles*. Fontaine, whose influence was greater than ever, imposed his own architectural ideas and taste for classical ornament. The reaction against a *meuble d'apparat*, monumental and exaggeratedly formal, is as yet hardly noticeable, in spite of Louis XVIII's genuine desire to live in informal and comfortable surroundings.

The innovations of this period issue from entirely different quarters. The aristocracy who had succeeded in getting back to their homes were not so lucky as the king; they had not found their family seats ready furnished and were therefore obliged to set about buying new furniture. Naturally they called upon the manufacturers they had known before fleeing into exile, and who had managed to survive the political turmoil; Bellanger, Dugourc, Lemarchand and Jacob-Desmalter were chosen to interpret the wishes of this clientèle and to resume the traditions of the old régime once more. These clever craftsmen created fresh models, at the same time bearing in mind the achievements of the preceding twenty-five years; they produced furniture that was no longer cold nor rigid, nor relied for its decoration solely on bronze mounts superimposed on sombre mahogany. Little by little, light native woods challenged the popularity of exotic woods; dainty, attractive garlands and bead chains staged a come-back in decoration; even the classical motifs became more human; finally, curved ornamentation dared once more to soften straight lines. This style of furniture, at once ancient

and modern, held infinite charm in the eyes of exiles return-
ing to their homes after so long an absence. Here more than
anywhere is the word 'Restoration' justified.

The aristocracy represented an extremely small clientèle,
and one whose fortunes had been drastically reduced. The
bulk of orders, therefore, came from a new section of society:
the middle classes. What are the aspirations of this part of the
population from whom – and this is quite unprecedented in
the development of a new style – artists must take their cue
from now on? These new customers have only a mediocre
appreciation of the arts but they are guided by common sense;
weary from so many national disasters and wars, they long
for practical, comfortable furniture; in any case they are
limited by the size of their homes. Instead of private mansions,
they live in rented apartments – better arranged but more
cramped. It is not that they are prejudiced in any way against
the Napoleonic style, but they want furniture suitable for a
sedentary family life.

Thus, alongside the luxurious pieces still being made, we see
quantities of excellently finished, unpretentious furniture:
because of its small size it is easy to move around; since it is
made in native wood it is relatively cheap; its structure may
lack purity but its lines are none the less often simple and
attractive. In any case, the new style is definitely not tainted
with that sombre austerity inherent in Napoleonic furniture.

Lastly, in addition to the trends which we might describe as
'classical', there emerges an ostentatious, grossly affected
style which is partly responsible for Restoration furniture's
bad reputation. In all periods of history there have been
designers who filled whole albums with outlandish designs in
order to attract customers by reason of their novelties and
fads. Furniture designs by Du Cerceau, Pineau or Percier
can be no less far-fetched than those by La Mésangère, Bance
or Muidebled. In every period craftsmen have been found
who were willing to translate the *ornemanistes'* crazy fantasies
into real pieces of furniture, but such pieces go out of fashion
very quickly, and often are destroyed by the next generation.
The period we are concerned with is a case in point; a number
of creations have come down to us which are directly inspired
by Bance's *Recueil de Décoration Intérieure*, published in 1828,

Charles Muidebled's *Vademecum du Tapissier*, published in 1835, or Pierre de La Mésangère's (1761–1831) *Meubles et Objets de Goût*. While some excellent 'classical' pieces of furniture were still being made, these, and other less well-known design books, offer a collection of pieces that are amusing but in doubtful taste. There existed at that time a wealthy clientèle which could not, however, pretend to any aesthetic education and which caused some curious *ensembles* to be made. Those people who had profited outrageously by the Revolutionary upheaval and the imperial wars thought they could attract attention by the way their houses were furnished, and thus put themselves on an equal footing with the aristocracy and the old-established middle classes.

The Restoration, indeed, was full of happy inventions, and the furniture of this period is not purely and simply a bastardised version of Empire furniture as we have judged it to be for several generations past. Furniture made between 1815 and 1830 does have certain characteristics that enable experts to date it accurately, but its structural form, very similar to that of the Empire, has been the subject of unfortunate confusion. Some superb Restoration pieces have been attributed to the Empire, but nearly all their minor, though characteristic, details share the legacy of both periods.

In spite of all this, we hesitate to talk of a Restoration style. The furniture lacks the cohesion and general harmony that would have resulted from a unanimous, common approach to art adopted by an *élite* of taste. There were some enlightened art lovers and talented *ébénistes* living between 1815 and 1830, but once they no longer felt bound by a single doctrine, each man worked as the spirit moved him. Is it perhaps this individualism in art that has recently caused us to take a fresh look at Restoration furniture?

2 | Technique and Decoration

▶ *Technique*

The technical perfection of Restoration furniture has often been applauded. It is the last period before furniture manu-

xxxiii *Round Table, Restoration Period*

facture was taken over by machine tools. These artisans had nothing to learn about veneering, marquetry and inlay-work. Craftsmen's equipment had improved, the old traditions that obtained before the guilds were abolished were revived. A great deal of water had gone under the bridge since 1789 and two styles of decoration had come and gone, but it is nevertheless true that only twenty-five years earlier a would-be *maître menuisier-ébéniste* had to serve a long apprenticeship and produce a masterpiece before being admitted to the inner sanctum of the guild. Men who have been quoted as the best furniture-makers round about 1820 all went through this thorough technical training; they took great pains to supply their customers with fine, well-constructed furniture.

Quality is not the only point in favour of Restoration furniture; its variety of technical processes does it just as much credit. Under the Empire some techniques were deliberately abandoned simply because they did not fit in with the requirements of Napoleonic art. Restoration *ébénistes* on the contrary reveal highly eclectic tastes: they successfully reintroduced all the woodwork skills that had been cultivated during the eighteenth century.

Consequently the almost non-existent mouldings on post-Revolution furniture come back into fashion again. Carving reappears on solid wood furniture; under the Empire moulding and carving had been relegated to wooden seats; we must admit, moreover, that this carving was distressingly mean and arid. At the same time the Empire had gone to the other extreme and allowed carving to get out of hand – seat- and table-legs had become thick and heavy with an invasion of figures carved in the round (see Chap. I, p. 26). The Restoration on the other hand sees carving restored to its true function: to decorate but not to modify structural form.

Marquetry was another technique that had nearly become extinct. From 1790 to 1800 *ébénistes* were forced through economic difficulties to work at top speed at very little profit; as marquetry was a lengthy and expensive decorative process it could only be applied to exceptional pieces. The Empire had settled for uniform mahogany veneers. The Restoration takes up again with tradition. However, its artists are not content with making mere reproductions of Louis XV or

xxxiv *Guéridon Table, Louis-Philippe*

Louis XVI marquetry designs. They not only discover new motifs but also employ hitherto untried colour combinations by using native woods. The effects they achieve are quite different because woods like ash, olive, satinwood and box now begin to feature in marquetry patterns.

Ebénistes turn their attention, however, primarily to inlay-work. This very old process (see Chap. I, p. 26) was hardly used at all in the eighteenth century, but now it reaches heights of popularity and technical perfection that have never been equalled since. Restrained, stylised motifs (kingwood on a light coloured wood like maple; box or satinwood on a dark wood like purplewood) are firmly embedded into the base-wood; neither heat, cold nor humidity can ever cause them to part company because the wood inlaid is so firmly welded on to the carcase that it becomes almost an integral part of the decorated panel.

Lastly, veneers show a whole new range of colours. With the fall of the Empire this trend towards bright colours is specially marked. Until 1820 most furniture was still made in mahogany. Some *ébénistes*, like Puteaux or Jeanselme, continue to adhere to it but others, like Verner or Lemarchand, were bold enough to show *meubles de luxe* in maple or walnut as early as the industrial exhibition in 1823. Jacob-Desmalter clings loyally to Empire traditions in most of his work but he is not afraid to experiment with new effects: he puts forward some furniture in ash for the 1819 exhibition.

This new taste in native woods for high-class *ébénisterie* probably stemmed from the economic conditions created by the Continental blockade and later by the 1815 treaties; but even the acute difficulties of importation combined with the high price of exotic woods would not in themselves have brought about a new trend in furniture design had the customers themselves not taken a strong fancy to light, gay colours and thus encouraged the *ébénistes* in their experiments. The Duchesse de Berry, the only member of the royal family capable of any artistic initiative, placed orders in about 1820 with the Mathias brothers for a suite of furniture lacquered white to go in her drawing-room.

With pressure of new demands now put on them, *ébénistes* were able to reveal the full glory of woods which, until then, had been treated as poor relations. Blessed with faultless good taste and a thorough understanding of each wood's decorative possibilities, furniture-manufacturers exploited the delicate rose tints in ash, the bird's-eye grain in thuya, the watered figure in plane, the knots in elm, the pale tones of sycamore, the amber or grey tones in maple, the root of box, etc. The *ébéniste*'s art no longer consists in searching out rare varieties of exotic woods but in discovering the beautiful, subtle shades in common woods. The way in which the wood is sawn can often do much to achieve a decorative effect. Wood is now no longer sawn only with the grain – it is also cut against the grain or in flitches (see Chap. I, p. 26). Roots, burrs and particularly knotted parts of the tree are all used. In this way one single variety of wood can offer tremendous possibilities.

No more do we see the strict division between veneering and working in solid wood that obtained in the eighteenth century; solid and veneered furniture is largely made in the same woods and artisans apply themselves to either technique at will. Veneering also reaches such perfection that we have to study a piece of furniture at very close quarters before we can say by which process it has been made. The manufacturer is always guided by the final result. If he cannot achieve the decorative effect he wants with a swirling figure in solid wood, he now has enough knowledge of wood-working techniques to use burrs and roots, which he will of course be forced to treat as veneers. Furniture takes on a new look through its bold colour contrasts which are entirely due to skilful use of common woods.

Unfortunately, this pioneer attempt, which could have given a fresh boost to the whole art of furniture-making, was not followed up. As early as 1830, the era of imitation and the mock-antique puts a stop to decorative experiments. The machine age, which came in about mid-century, made imitation easy and further contributed to check any original creative impulse.

It is not long before technical perfection comes to be mistaken for good artistry. Such furniture is marvellously well constructed, but its decoration has been appropriated from past centuries. We have had to wait until the twentieth century for our modern craftsmen to be enlightened enough to bring new life into furniture-manufacture by using new woods – notably exotic ones – and new techniques. The Restoration was the last period of original invention; for almost a century since, designers, decorators and *ébénistes* have turned to the past and lived by imitation and *pastiche*.

▶ *Decoration*

The cold symbolic decoration of the Empire period undergoes some rapid transformations. Quite apart from structural form and bright colours, the Restoration looks for a note of light-heartedness and informality in decoration. The mythological and fantastic animals that the Empire was so fond of beat a hasty retreat: chimeras, griffons, dolphins and seahorses are still to be found, but they are smaller and do not play so important a part in the decoration. Arm-chairs have simple volutes for their arm supports instead of winged genii or some other weird and wonderful monsters. Applied bronze ornaments are much rarer than they were under the Empire; mythological figures such as Fame, Fortune and the Seasons are replaced by less formal motifs: cherubs, lyres, swans, or just the inevitable palmette, introduce a discreet light touch here and there into an otherwise very sombre façade.

The range of ornament is meagre because the veneers provide an adequate decoration in themselves. Inlay-work is interesting for its colour contrasts rather than its stylised motifs. The artists' chief concern is not to overload their furniture with decoration, since their customers want uncluttered lines and sober ornamentation. Thus the ornament on a secretaire, for instance, may be reduced to a simple moulding, peg-top feet and three keyhole plates in bronze gilt. A table-top might for instance be decorated with an oval motif so extremely stylised that we have to look at it some time before recognising a rosette surrounded by two palmettes and six bouquets of flowers.

There is not much variety therefore in decoration. The palmette, taken from the *Directoire* and Empire, crops up everywhere and in many different forms (see Plate xxxiii). Sometimes it is so highly stylised that we can barely recognise it at all. The lyre is not a particularly new motif either; we find it inlaid, carved, or made into a bronze mount and even table-legs. A few other elements lifted from the decorative repertoire of the old régime undergo very slight modifications. These are the egg-and-dart, rosette, pearl beading, ribbon band, garland of foliage, floral scrollwork and the like. Marquetry and inlay-work employ various geometrical designs where squares, lozenges, rectangles, circles and ellipses appear in countless combinations that help to show off the variety of colours in the wood.

Under the Restoration decoration subsided into the background except for a few specially commissioned pieces such as the table presented to Charles X by the city of Paris (see Plate XXXIII). Elements taken from other styles – rosettes at the intersection of cross-stretchers, keyhole plates – are affected by clearly distinguishable but unoriginal changes.

3 | The Different Types of Furniture

▶ *Seat Furniture*

The farther away we get from the Empire, the lighter and less rectilinear seats become. They are more comfortable and easier to move. Many different types of seat are made, either slightly modified imitations of the Empire or reproductions of models belonging to a more distant age.

The chairs and arm-chairs which we might call *sièges de reception*, are not very different from those Percier designed in about 1810. The padded, upholstered back may be straight or slightly rolled-over; the rear legs are sabre-form; the front legs are square in section, curved forwards instead of being straight; chimeras or winged genii continue to be used for a short time as arm-supports. This kind of seat is sometimes painted white and picked out in gold.

This type of chair is soon adapted for common use. The back is curved to fit better round the back of a seated person; it slopes slightly as a concession to comfort. The upper traverse is no longer made up of a strictly rectilinear piece, but by two confronted volutes making a bow-shaped profile,

L

or simply by a rounded traverse. Whilst Etruscan-style legs are still in fashion, back legs are more splayed than they were under the Directory and the Empire, in order to make the seat firmer. Spindle and baluster legs make a quick comeback into fashion but they are not so elegant as in the early years of the century. Finally, after Charles X cabriole legs become common again.

The Restoration derives the fashion of pierced backs on chairs from the Empire, but proves to have less originality and imagination. The different types of back are limited. The commonest is that formed by a crosspiece or a rectangular panel filled in with trellis-work. After Charles X we also find motifs in the shape of a fan or one or two empty scallop shells. As under the Directory, the upper traverse is often hollowed out into a half-moon to serve as a hand-hold; alternatively a spindle linking the two back uprights may serve the same purpose.

The 'gondola' chair or arm-chair, whose appearance we noted under the Directory, rose to unprecedented heights of popularity. This is the type of chair which best fulfils the period's aspirations towards comfort and well-being. The back exactly follows the shape of a human back and the sides slope gently down to join a low seat. Swans and dolphins are still plentiful on specially high-class pieces, where they form arms separate from the seat. Legs are often fitted with castors, thus making this small seat highly mobile. There are also some seats for more specific purposes: some very interesting *fauteuils de bureau* for instance where the back is made of a carved or pierced round plaque.

Of the eighteenth-century sofa-type seats, the Empire retained only the *canapé* and the *méridienne*. Both continue to be used under the Restoration. Until about 1820, any modifications to the *méridienne* are confined to ornamental details, but gradually the seat-rail is placed lower and lower until it turns into a base. The *canapé* develops in the same way. *Ottomanes* inherited from the old régime, *causeuses* and *dormeuses* that developed from the eighteenth-century *veilleuses*, and huge kidney-shaped divans are all covered with upholstery right down to the base and piled with cushions. Very few of these 'dust-traps' have survived the passage of time, but, judging by Devéria's lithographs, they must have been widely used. These capacious, comfortable seats mark the *tapissier*'s first victory over the *ébéniste*: under the Second Empire there is no wood to be seen at all on some chairs (see Glossary).

▶ *Beds*

If we were to judge by the plethora of names used by furniture-makers of the day we might think there were many different kinds of beds made. In fact, they may be reduced to two types, as they were under the Empire: the bed with rectilinear uprights in the form of pilasters or columns, and the 'boat' bed. One of the finest examples of the latter, made by Lemarchand in satinwood inlaid with ebony, is in the *Musée des Arts Décoratifs*. It is typical of the high quality craftsmanship of this period: light-toned wood, stylised and inlaid decoration, perfect execution.

▶ *General Furniture*

Furniture in general takes many and varied forms. The Empire style commode with three drawers is still in constant production until about 1820–5. After that it becomes gradually lighter; it loses its pilasters, its columns and its bronze accessories; it is no longer made in mahogany but in light wood inlaid with a dark, restrained decoration. Enclosed *secrétaires* evolve in the same way. Almost imperceptibly, bureaux – whether they are *bureaux plats*, *bureaux à cylindre* or *à dos d'âne* – grow more complex and heavy. Often they have eight feet and drawers right down to the ground. The flat tops of these bureaux were encumbered with a multiplicity of small shelves for keeping papers, and sometimes books, in order. Even so, they do not expand under the Restoration to such large proportions as they later reach under Louis-Philippe, though they are not so elegant as the eighteenth-century ones.

Dining-tables are also very massive. Their legs are sometimes reminiscent of the Empire: winged or terminal figures, swans, cornucopiae, or, more simply and more frequently,

lions' feet with powerful protruding claws. Lyres enjoy an un-
equalled popularity – witness the table presented to Charles X
by the City of Paris (see Plate xxxiii). A whole crowd of
other smaller tables, gracefully and skilfully made, go to fill
Restoration suites: circular or oval *tricoteuses* and *vide-poches*,
tables à secrets with hidden drawers, dining or tea tables in the
shape of a *guéridon* standing on a central column or tripod
and other tables intended for specific purposes: work tables,
tables à coiffer, gaming tables.

The Restoration *ébénistes* showed themselves in no way inferior to eighteenth-century *ébénistes* in their creation of
many different forms, in their search for new types of furniture
that would make daily life easier and would make their
clients' homes pleasant and comfortable places. *Ebénistes* were
impelled by the small size of the new rooms to devise furniture
that could be adapted to several different uses. These dual-
purpose pieces are very interesting. Our modern craftsmen,
so adept at this type of design, have in fact done no more
than revive old ideas.

In addition to these numerous pieces, we should mention
certain legacies handed down by the Empire which the
Restoration did little to alter: *psychés* (see Glossary) and toilet
mirrors, bedside tables and wash-stands. Console tables,
similar to Empire ones at the start of the Restoration, by
about 1825 have volutes and cornucopiae for their legs.

It may be that Restoration furniture has long been decried
because it is hard to define. Its experimentation and un-
settled phase of development conceal its undeniable good
qualities from those who only make a superficial study of it.
Nevertheless this practical, comfortable, logically and perfectly constructed furniture is not without elegance or charm.
Its quiet lines, its light tones of wood and its multiplicity of
shapes make it a worthy successor to furniture in the
eighteenth-century tradition.

4 | The July Monarchy

This brief period marks a decisive turn in the art of furniture-
making. The first Restoration had wrought a clever com-

promise between eighteenth-century art and the demands of a new society. Artisans of the Louis-Philippe era break with the customs of the old régime and create furniture which, besides expressing artistic theories, reflects exactly the current literary, social, and even political aspirations of an extremely mixed society.

That staggering transformation which aims at replacing human labour by machines throws technical processes into disorder as well as aesthetic ideas. Artists are now confronted with a completely fresh problem: that of evolving an industrial art. We know that these industrial artists were at a loss to find their right medium for nearly a whole century. Machines had become a social necessity: the middle classes, summoned overnight to fill high appointments, had to set about furnishing their homes quickly, without the help of family heirlooms. There was no time to order uniquely styled and exquisitely hand-made furniture from artisans; the ordinary individual had to choose his furniture from one of the large specialist stores that began to spring up in Paris round about this time. Naturally companies like these offered their customers mass-production pieces; such rapid manufacture of identical pieces was due solely to the introduction of machine tools.

The current political theories encouraged the sale of mass-production furniture: the equality of private citizens was very much a problem of the day; fine furniture previously reserved for the privileged classes had to be put within the means of as many people as possible. However, mass production is not yet a synonym for inferior quality: woods are still carefully and competently selected. The artisan may use machines for cutting veneers, marquetry patterns and inlays, but the glueing and finishing are still done by hand and as skilfully as ever; technically, the results are equal to those obtained under the old régime. Unfortunately the same does not apply to carved decoration: work done by machine produces sharp, hard contours which had never been the outcome of work done by hand. This defect is still scarcely noticeable in Louis-Philippe's reign when artisans used to correct machine imperfections, but it is much more evident under the Second Empire and the Third Republic.

Between 1830 and 1848 there still existed a large number of craftsmen who, from childhood upwards, were wont to make their furniture without recourse to machines. In cases where they had to compete for speed with others who used the new processes, and were themselves obliged to enlist the aid of machines in order to earn a living, they did not forfeit all artistic feeling. Their role had not yet been reduced to that of a machine operative, who, in the very near future, would merely put together various pieces of wood turned out by a machine, and who would not be supposed, let alone able, to use his own initiative in modifying any part of the work. Working conditions, however, changed so drastically that some highly skilled *ébénistes* lost heart on account of the new methods and preferred to close down their workshops. In 1849 Alphonse Jacob-Desmalter abandoned his trade.

Since machines removed a good deal of the artisan's own initiative, designers had to be called on to supply models that could be mass-produced quickly. Original ideas begin to be rare; for everyday furniture artisans are generally content to copy and re-copy existing forms. Since 1815 there had been no properly clear-cut pattern of development; hundreds of different trends clash, follow on and replace each other. The immediate result of this dearth of inspiration is a return to past styles. The start of the antique dealers' 'reign' adds to the indescribable confusion amidst which ornamental art struggles for survival. There is no leading light, among all the architects and decorators, able to compel universal recognition and stem the course of all these conflicting and fleeting trends.

Henceforth, instead of adapting form to suit custom and convenience, people furnished their houses like museums according to the latest vogue; but since archaeological finds were still very limited and economic depression made cheap mass-production imperative, the copies we see are merely tame reproductions of old models. Luckily this artificial, arbitrary method of furnishing was not adopted everywhere. It was restricted to a very small section of high society, but it was not without some influence on furniture in general use.

▶ *The Designers' Role*

Designers now play an all-important part in furniture design. For generations *ébénistes* had taken their inspiration from the work of *ornemanistes*, but as soon as furniture design was expected to revive a style several centuries old, it became absolutely essential that the work produced should be based on solid documentation. The designers were the only ones in a position to go and discover models in old buildings, look in print-rooms or archives, and bring back from oblivion the forms and decoration of the past. Under Louis-Philippe and during the first fifteen years of the Second Empire, the art of previous centuries is used only as a source of inspiration for general themes; no one as yet would dream of making facsimiles. The working methods of Aimé Chenavard, the most famous *ornemaniste* of the period, are typical in this respect. He already wielded great influence and his talent was well recognised long before he published his *Nouveau recueil d'ornements* (1833–5). As far back as 1830 he was appointed artistic director of the *Manufacture Royale de Sèvres*, and the only really worthwhile arts review of the day, *L'Artiste*, asked for frontispieces by him as well as others like Tony Johannot, Célestin Nanteuil and Clerget. According to the Comte de Laborde, Chenavard 'worked like a hornet'. He plundered the ornamental repertoire of all countries and all ages for motifs which he crammed into his chaotic and overcharged designs. In his hands, not a single motif is allowed to keep its original outline or its right and proper proportions. A whole group of satellite designers, Chenavard's pupils and others, whose names are nearly all unknown to us, continue to pillage indiscriminately every document they can lay hands on. As well as Gothic and Louis XV, long forgotten Assyrian, Chinese, Egyptian and Greek ornaments are dragged out into the open again. Furniture manufacturers only have to glance at one of these all too numerous albums and they start producing furniture in some ridiculous Neo-Gothic or Neo-Egyptian fancy dress.

Thus it was that the 'Cathedral' style emerged from the distant past, a long time even before the Bourbon dynasty fell. By a curious coincidence, old French styles were imitated more or less in chronological order. The Neo-Gothic reached its height between 1830 and 1833, but the beginnings of this vogue date back as far as 1821. Hittorf and Leconte had filled the whole interior of Notre-Dame with medieval hangings for the baptism of the Duke of Bordeaux. A few years later in 1824 when Charles X was crowned, Reims Cathedral was hung with 'Gothick' tapestries. From this time onwards the 'Troubadour' style gained ground by leaps and bounds both in literature and art. The ball given by the Duchesse de Berry, at which she appeared disguised as Mary Queen of Scots, encouraged designers to exploit this fashion. Furniture followed suit in the prevailing taste. It was swamped in a 'flamboyant' decoration, superimposed on a very ordinary framework. Rosettes, quatrefoils and blind or open 'window tracery' are used to decorate seat-backs and the doors of the larger pieces. Pinnacles, even crenellations, machicolations and gargoyles provide cumbersome trimmings on these extraordinary 'Gothick' creations, giving a fantastic and theatrical appearance to this utterly conventional furniture.

The 'Cathedral' style represents a momentary whim exclusive to artists and their rich clients. It was soon outdated. Lack of documentation – it was impossible to find authentic pieces even in those days – meant that the Neo-Gothic style was restricted to mere reproduction right from the start, and by the time Duchatel had induced the State to buy the Du Sommerard collection in 1843 and had set up the *Musée de Cluny*, 'Romantic' furniture had long gone out of fashion.

Consequently, another theme had to be found. The deplorable habit of imitation had now become so firmly engrained in artists' minds that creating something new simply meant drawing inspiration from another period or another country. At the 1834 industrial exhibition some of the best furniture-manufacturers showed the need for innovation. Werner and Bellangé both exhibited 'Chinese' furniture alongside Neo-Gothic pieces. Grohé, whilst offering his public some outstanding examples of rosewood furniture with 'Gothick' inlays, also tried the experiment of some Neo-Egyptian pieces so exquisitely made that Princess Marie, the

xxxv *Bed, Second Empire*

king's daughter, selected them for her own use. Other
designers turned to Persia and Islam. They cast about in vain
for a style that would appeal to public taste and become
established. *Meubles de luxe*, which had of necessity to be
novelties, now become lost in a wilderness of strange, fantastic
shapes and mixed methods of carving in which all the different
styles are jumbled together. The album Leconte edited in
1838 is symptomatic of this confusion. Here we have a team
of designers like Devergise, Reynard and Couder offering
their public the incredibly incoherent *Mélange d'Ornements
Divers*.

However, amongst so many trials and failures, the 'Renaissance' style was lucky enough to have a talented champion in
the person of Michel Liénard who exerted a lasting influence
on the evolution of furniture. Unlike Chenavard, Liénard
devoted himself to one style alone and made a thorough
study of it. He went to great lengths to find the best examples
in façades of Renaissance Chateaux, furniture, and sixteenth-
century prints. Moreover, he was blessed with a natural
aptitude for composition; his furniture is systematically constructed. Although Neo-Renaissance furniture was already
being made in 1840 on the basis of Liénard's designs, most of
his work belongs to the Second Empire.

▶ *Furniture in General Use*

These products of designers' fantasies were not without some
influence on ordinary furniture. However, the furniture that
most of Louis-Philippe's contemporaries possessed was neither
Neo-Gothic nor Neo-Renaissance, still less 'Chinese' or
'Egyptian': it was a direct continuation of the earlier Restoration, though there are a few modifications we should note. At
first, the Louis-Philippe period shows a resolute disregard for
the lighter-toned woods. Dark woods such as rosewood and
ebony and those dyed black such as pear and beech steal
the show completely. Now that furniture is mass-produced
we find a great many identical pieces. Furniture framework is
overcome by a universal heaviness; seat legs grow thicker:
they are either curved or bulbous at the top; others are
machine-turned and fluted into a peg-top. The cornices above

the top drawers are decorated with broad, bold *doucine* mouldings. Seldom do we come across delicate ornament or detail: bronze mounts are a rarity; the machine age and the need to bring democracy into furniture are responsible for this impoverishment.

On the other hand, the number of essential articles of furniture in the home grows less with the invention of some ingenious combination pieces. Thus tall, massive commodes could be made very versatile, depending on what devices the manufacturer had recourse to. As a general rule, they simply conceal a set of drawers behind their doors; this type is known as a *commode à l'anglaise*, but there are some commodes where the top drawer is left showing and this can serve as a desk when pulled out. Other commodes have a toilet table hidden under the flat top. Lastly, certain commodes fitted with an upper, glass-paned, section can be turned into book-cabinets.

The *semainier* or *chiffonnier* is an extremely useful piece which to some extent replaces the *commode à tiroirs* of previous periods. It stands tall and narrow, and contains seven superposed drawers which can contain a multitude of objects without taking up too much room.

The *armoire* is not so rich in fresh possibilities. Furthermore, the *armoire à glace* (mirror wardrobe) is not a Louis-Philippe creation, though in this period it comes much more into general use and constitutes an indispensable article of bedroom furniture. It is usually veneered in mahogany, tall, wide and generously moulded. A drawer at the base sometimes balances the moulded cornice on top.

The *écran pupitre* (desk with fitted screen) is a clever Louis-Philippe invention. This is a small, light, mobile secretaire fitted with a flap that makes it possible to write while sitting in front of the fire, at the same time shielding one's face with a small screen.

Tables are round; the most typical ones are made up of a heavy top resting on a single wooden pedestal leg, turned, and reeded, with a bulbous swelling in the middle (see Plate xxxiv). This type of leg splays out flat on to a triangular or rectangular base, which in turn rests on lions' paws or castors.

Smaller tables, rectangular or square, are fitted with folding flaps in order to economise on space in the now cramped dwellings. A whole series of small tables continues to be made: *dessertes* (side-tables or dumb-waiters), *travailleuses* (work-tables) and *jardinières* (plant stands).

It would seem, therefore, that Louis-Philippe *ébénistes* strained their wits to produce practical furniture which would meet the requirements of domestic comfort and which would at the same time take up a minimum amount of space.

Seats are also typical of this age when comfort is considered more important than aesthetics. We may note the appearance of the 'Voltaire' arm-chair at this point: set on short legs, it is deep-seated, has a high, button-upholstered back and high, padded arms. Possibly it was inspired by the Louis XIV arm-chair, from which it takes its rectangular back. Comfort is assured by supple lines: it is carefully curved to fit round the small of a person's back.

The small *crapaud* (tub easy-chair) with no visible *ébénisterie* to it at all, and various capacious *canapés* take their place alongside light chairs with pierced backs and all-enveloping, curved 'gondola' arm-chairs.

Although it produced extravagant pieces in bad taste and other hastily mass-produced furniture heralding the age of cheap, shoddy goods, the Louis-Philippe period did succeed in continuing the furniture traditions of bygone periods and it turned out some simple, strong, comfortable and entirely praiseworthy articles of furniture.

The fact remains, however, that the Citizen King's eighteen years' reign represents a critical phase in the history of French furniture, when we see it in the throes of a definitive transformation. Henceforth every manufacturer has to grapple with two quite new problems: if he is to stay in business he must undertake cheap mass-production; at the same time he must make copies of whatever old-fashioned style happens to be popular with the public at the moment. This frightful mania for everything antique that started under Louis-Philippe had endless repercussions. Nothing could have been more detrimental to experimentation with new styles than this anomaly of using obsolete forms. Decorators were so hide-bound by this new conception of art that for fifty years no attempt was made to break free from imitation and search elsewhere for the right forms that would once more bring the art of furniture-making back to life.

| THE SECOND EMPIRE

The last kings of France took almost no interest whatsoever
in the art produced during their reigns, and Napoleon III
attached no greater importance to the decorative arts than
did his predecessors. He was utterly unfitted for the role of
patron of the arts, either by virtue of his personal taste or his
acquired knowledge; he left all initiative in that respect to
the Empress or his ministers. Yet he had a greater influence
than we are inclined to suppose. He wished to surround himself with a dazzling court that would enhance the prestige of
the French Crown; he was also impelled by a general concern for social and economic stability to foster the growing
national industry. The decorative arts benefited from these
two items on the Imperial programme and immense efforts
were made to promote all branches of industrial art. Needless
to say, there was no general unified policy. Also, despite some
excellent experimental work, successful results were few and
far between. The Empress was not altogether lacking in
taste but, unfortunately, in spite of her love for magnificence,
she had a tiresome tendency to be satisfied with hybrid
furniture derived from the art of the past, and her numerous
orders never provoked any attempt at a progressive, living
art. Thus, throughout the Second Empire we find excellent
ébénistes engrossed in making an almost complete inventory of
all the forms and decorative styles used by their predecessors
over the previous 500 years. This 'review' of furniture history
renders all original talent ineffectual and stifles every attempt

at innovation; after twenty years of imitation and *pastiche* it was inevitably more difficult than ever before for furniture to become emancipated from such obsolete forms. Although some clear-sighted critics proclaimed as early as the 1889 Exhibition that French decorative art was heading in the wrong direction, nearly half a century elapsed before manufacturers and customers were convinced that valid themes of inspiration should be sought elsewhere than in the past.

The period we are about to study covers a much wider span than the eighteen years of Napoleon III's effective reign. Those documents which the Second Empire *ébénistes* drew on so extensively were published long before 1848. Examples of all the styles could not only be found in Chenavard's pattern books, which we have already mentioned, but also in those by Feuchère, or in notes made by various artists such as Devergise, Couder, Ovide Reynard and others, later compiled by publishers into huge collections such as the *Mélanges d'Ornements Divers* which appears under the name of Leconte in 1838 or the *Repertoire de l'Ornemaniste* published by Blaisot in 1841. There also existed a whole host of designers whose talents varied enormously and whose work is difficult to distinguish and characterise; with the financial support of several publishing houses, these artists published a multitude of designs which they had shamelessly copied – without acknowledging the fact – from artists of bygone ages. Unfortunately these pattern books had an extraordinarily long-lasting influence, proved by the fact that the same books still served as a basis for all furniture made in the *Faubourg Saint-Antoine* as late as 1900.

The Second Empire has therefore left a deep impression on the art of furniture-making, probably because there is an undeniable unity underlying its incongruous appearance: its richness, its brilliance, its sumptuous appearance and vivid colours tend to make one forget that this is a mode of imitation; and, moreover, it refrains from being servile. In fact, Napoleon III's contemporaries never tired, as the fanatical twentieth-century antique-hunters did, to make identical reconstructions. The greatest factor that brought Napoleon III furniture into disrepute was low-price mass-production, intended to put pseudo-Riesener and pseudo-Boulle within the reach of everyone's pocket. This era of shoddy goods, imitation and cheap glitter flooded the market with furniture whose bronze mounts were gilded by galvanisation and whose mechanically carved decoration transformed pure Renaissance models into disagreeable caricatures.

▶ *Materials*

High-class furniture, however, is still marvellously well constructed and the finest materials are used. Now that mahogany has fallen from the position of honour it held since the time of Louis XVI, it can serve for furniture in general use. Purplewood and ebony are also most popular. These sombre black woods make a superb background to set off the ornaments and the warm, vivid colours of the draperies used to decorate windows or cover seats. On more modest pieces, pearwood and beechwood continue to be dyed black as imitation ebony. Oak is restricted to Neo-Renaissance furniture where carving plays an important part.

In fact, in many instances the wood merely provides a foundation: inlays are made out of precious woods (kingwood, tulipwood), metals (silver, steel), animal products (mother-of-pearl, tortoise-shell, ivory) or even cubes of coloured stone in mosaic patterns; we also see inset porcelain plaques, enamel, japanned or varnished tin and even dried flowers pressed under glass. Lastly, the dark wood is itself occasionally painted with decorative motifs, notably flowers, in very bright colours. Elaborately wrought bronze mounts make a further contribution towards masking the wooden uprights, friezes and cornices.

Wood often disappears from view on seats under a profusion of upholstery fabrics. However, some seats were made with the wood still in evidence, but in these cases the wood was varnished, gilt or painted. A highly specialised and very old technique was successfully revived under Napoleon III, giving rise to a variety of light and charming seats. These seats have their backs made of *carton deguisé*. The use of paper pulp, made into a paste and then moulded into shape, had already been known as early as the sixteenth century. However, it was not until 1772 that Henry Clay took this process a stage farther by having the idea of covering the *papier mâché* with a layer of lacquer or varnish. By adding straw or hay glued together with pitch or resin, this new material could be pressed into a metal mould and sawn, polished or filed down. After that it could be used to make into furniture. The gracefully curved backs that resulted harmonised remarkably well with the sombre, dazzlingly ornamented furniture of the second Napoleonic era. Various light occasional chairs (*chaise volantes*) suitable for wide crinolines were also made at this time.

► *Decoration and Structure*

It may seem strange to speak of 'Second Empire' decoration when all its ingredients are taken from old styles. However, it is true to say that *ornemanistes* chose a certain number of motifs from each ornamental repertoire and to some extent specialised in them.

When Prince Napoleon became Emperor, the Renaissance, promoted by Liénard, was the style foremost in fashion. However, the Second Empire retained only a few motifs from the arsenal of Renaissance decoration; these motifs were then distorted, first by the *ornemaniste*'s pencil and secondly by the *ébéniste*'s scissors. Furthermore, Neo-Renaissance decoration was very soon confined to a limited number of specific pieces.

The standard forms of table-legs are sphinxes, lions with gaping jaws and powerful claws, chimeras, etc. On simpler models, the legs are reduced to two heavily moulded supports, linked by a traverse. Panels on *buffets* are usually decorated with hunting or fishing trophies tied together into bundles and suspended by ribbon-knots, which in turn hang from the gaping jaws of grimacing mascarons. We also find scenes of pheasants in cornfields or ducks among reeds carved in lower relief. The uprights on *buffets* and book-cabinets are decorated with caryatids that are too heavy and too protruding, and with massive allegorical figures and little angels whose long tumbling tresses give them a somewhat dismal appearance. Cartouches, pearl beading, interlaced patterns and elaborate mouldings are scattered everywhere. The high, straight backs

XXXVI *Jewel Cabinet, Second Empire*

of chairs are lavishly carved with identical motifs; legs turn into pilasters linked by traverses.

Neo-Renaissance decoration is thus sadly lacking in inspiration; its cold and melancholy atmosphere contrasts strangely with the wealth of exuberance and joy found in true Renaissance decoration. Nevertheless, the best *ébénistes* such as Grohé, Henri Fourdinois and Tahan all vied with each other in reproducing those pseudo-Renaissance ornamental designs which Liénard, Clerget, Klagmann and many others had previously published in an attempt to imitate the sixteenth-century French, German or Italian artists. The vogue for this pseudo-Renaissance style was an exceptional one and only the Empress's taste for pseudo-Riesener succeeded in halting, though not in extinguishing, this trend. Neo-Renaissance furniture continued to be produced almost without a break from 1835 to 1900.

The Louis XIV style also had its devotees; both periods were very similar as regards their decorative tendencies. Under the 'Grand Monarque', as under Napoleon III, the Court and high society liked to live in an exaggeratedly grand and resplendent setting. Thus the rigid, formal seventeenth-century seats easily fitted in with the furniture of the Imperial salons. The woods and gilt bronze mounts harmonised wonderfully well with the dazzling colours of the hangings. It was quite natural to make copies of André-Charles Boulle's work; its sumptuous overall effect, its use of dark ebony, the flashy brilliance of its brass, ivory and tortoise-shell marquetry – all were qualities that appealed to Napoleon III's contemporaries. Some *ébénistes* specialised in making *bas d'armoire*, corner-cupboards, book-cabinets, small tables in ebony or – failing ebony – pearwood dyed black, covered in marquetry designs which are often composed of steel and imitation tortoise-shell as well as brass and pewter. Wasmus and Frederic Roux appear to have been the chief manufacturers of furniture 'in the Boulle manner'.

The Louis XV style was copied to a far greater extent. Round about 1855 we see the triumph of the Pompadour style at the Paris Universal Exhibition. Second Empire artists found Rococo immensely attractive. They were not afraid of superfluous decoration and appeared to believe that

xxxvii *Chairs, Second Empire*

M

overloading a piece of furniture with ornament indicated riches and splendour. Simplicity and unity are concepts entirely foreign to these artists. Consequently, Baroque decoration runs riot on many pieces. The *coiffeuses, serre-bijoux* (jewel-cabinets), *bureaux de dame* and countless small tables – in short all the articles of bedroom furniture – rejoiced in a profusely carved *décor* which was full of movement and which smothered the framework of furniture with volutes, arabesques, flowers and shells. Catenacci designed some highly fanciful little pieces using every possible amusing, comic little device of Rococo decoration. Some table-legs also derive from the Louis XV style: small or console tables are supported by slender, curved *pieds-de-biche*. Psuedo-Louis XV is particularly applicable to seats. As usual, what we find are not exact copies, but old designs adapted to suit modern needs. The modifications apply in two respects. Firstly the old shapes are made more comfortable; seats are lower, their curved lines are more enveloping, their feet are fitted with castors and button upholstery replaces plain stuffed upholstery. Secondly, decoration is adapted to the new working methods: the use of machine tools forces moulding to become simpler and the range of decorative motifs to be more limited. On the other hand the taste for excessive decoration leads *ébénistes* to carve parts of a seat which were formerly left bare. Turning reigns supreme on countless occasional chairs with their slender, flimsy legs and pierced backs, either painted or gilt; they may look fragile but they are strong enough to stand up to any test when they come from the workshops of *ébénistes* like Henri Fourdinois.

A few years later the Neo-Pompeian style sees its hour of glory. In about 1860 Prince Jérome Napoléon asked his architect Charles Rossigneux to build and decorate a villa in the Neo-Greek style. This princely whim had no great repercussions on the general trends of furniture design. We merely see a few *guéridon* tables or pseudo-Roman arm-chairs occupying places of honour in exhibitions or artists' studios. Unlike all the free copies of antique styles that until then had been used to furnish the Imperial palaces, the Roman furniture designed for the Avenue Montaigne was as nearly as possible a reproduction, scientifically made from plaster casts. This experiment led nowhere. Despite its intense desire for learning, Second Empire society did not care to sacrifice its ease and comfort to satisfy archaeological demands.

However, it gradually became fashionable to reproduce antique styles accurately. In about 1865 the Empress was seized with a regular passion for everything that had been connected with Marie-Antoinette. She took Oeben's, Beneman's and Riesener's furniture out of store to furnish her apartments; she ordered copies of pieces made by the eighteenth-century *maîtres-ébénistes* for her personal use; some of the replicas ordered by the Empress were extremely accurate since the *ébénistes* of that time were technically just as skilled as their predecessors. Yet here the process of reproduction stops short. There was never any question of sacrificing comfort to the pleasure of living in rooms identical with Marie-Antoinette's. Although each individual commode, table, corner-cupboard, roll-top desk and *bonheur-du-jour* was made to look authentic down to the last detail, the *ensembles* which the Empress created had a certain incongruous charm; her pouffes, her button-upholstered seats fitted with fringes, tassels, lace trimmings and castors, her glowing, vividly coloured hangings round windows and doors, the rigid mouldings, the superimposed carving and the exaggeratedly glittering bronze mounts betray equally clearly the fact that this so-called Louis XVI is a purely fanciful Louis XVI.

A fashion with such exalted origins as this was naturally soon followed up and pseudo-Riesener furniture went into full-scale production. Grohé and Fourdinois still used rare woods for their private customers and made up impeccable marquetry patterns of tulipwood and kingwood, but the producers of shoddy pseudo-Riesener overlaid their badly constructed carcases of cheap white wood with ready-made mass-produced marquetry patterns. Thus with this 'Louis XVI/Empress' style we come to the end of the review of antique French styles.

In order to complete the picture, we should point out here that some pieces of furniture, notably panelled pieces, were inspired by fantastic Chinese-style designs; lacquered corner-cupboards and drop-front secretaires often feature painted mother-of-pearl decoration set into bronze Rococo frames.

We know by looking at the catalogues of various Universal Exhibitions that several manufacturers (Reiber, Boutemy, Raullin) specialised in Chinese-style decoration. Very few of these pieces are still in existence.

English styles also enjoyed a considerable vogue. We see some very rigid chairs with pierced backs inspired by Chippendale models. Such imitations represented a passing phase; they merely endorsed current trends. Those incorrigible *pasticheurs*, the *ébénistes* of the Second Empire, proved themselves incapable of creating a truly original style. Renewal simply meant for them a more or less faithful reproduction of furniture made in another age or another country.

1 | The Different Types of Furniture

Two new notions predominate in the furnishing of interiors: firstly, pieces of furniture copied from different styles may be placed together in the same room; secondly, the number of pieces is greatly increased and rooms are so overcrowded with furniture that it is difficult to navigate one's way through the labyrinth of small tables, occasional chairs and pouffes.

On the other hand, each antique style is allotted to one particular room in the apartment. Neo-Renaissance is the prescribed style for the dining-room, whilst pseudo-Boulle, inlaid or marquetry furniture, and gilt wood seat-furniture (imitation Louis XIV, Louis XV and Louis XVI) are arranged in state in the drawing-room. Button-upholstered pieces— a more intimate type of furniture – are allotted to the bedroom. The sombre, austere Neo-Classic style is often favoured in libraries and boudoirs. This segregation of styles is not strictly adhered to in practice. *Causeuses* and pouffes may well be set alongside *cabriolet* chairs in the drawing-room. The Pompadour-style *coiffeuse* also finds a home surrounded by softly cushioned button-upholstery.

It is practically impossible to list the pieces of furniture used under the Second Empire. We find ourselves confronted with three types: those pieces the *ébéniste* copies from an antique style and modernises in the belief that he is improving them; various new pieces (pouffe, umbrella-stand, etc.), and last but by no means least, scores of hybrid pieces which are impossible to catalogue under proper, stylistic headings because the manufacturers of the time concocted such odd mixtures: we might for instance come across a Louis XV seat decorated with pseudo-Boulle marquetry!

▶ *Cupboard Furniture*

Buffets, corner-cupboards, *commodes à l'anglaise* and *bas d'armoire* are made in the Neo-Renaissance, pseudo-Boulle and pseudo-Riesener styles. As usual, no style is copied down to the last detail. A rectilinear pseudo-Riesener *bas d'armoire* may for instance be attractively decorated with some fanciful motif which has no connection with the Louis XVI style, either in its design or in the materials used. The doors might also be decorated with a massive floral bouquet set in a capacious double-handled vase. Marble, porphyry, agate or cornelian inlaid into an ebony base are generally used for this kind of ornamentation.

A Boulle-style commode may very properly be decorated with brass and tortoise-shell marquetry on an ebony base, but this time the structure differs from what a Louis XIV *ébéniste* would have used. Octagonal-section columns flank the two rear uprights of the commode and the feet consist of spirally turned metal pieces.

Modifications made by *ébénistes* of the Second Empire sometimes apply to the materials used instead of the style adopted. For instance, a panel of a Louis XVI *commode à l'anglaise* would normally have been decorated with a floral bouquet. In the eighteenth century this bouquet would have been executed in various skilfully selected and veneered coloured woods. In the nineteenth century on the other hand, *ébénistes* used vividly coloured hard stones inlaid into the base-wood. We may also mention here that one Second Empire innovation consists in lining the insides of cupboard furniture with light-toned wood, mirrors, button upholstery or luxury fabrics such as satin.

▶ *Glass-paned Furniture*

Glass-paned furniture differs from other types only in the area of glass used. The small *vitrines, bas d'armoire* (greater in width than height) and the very big book-cabinets are generally made in rectilinear form. These articles of glass-paned furniture were extremely popular because they provided somewhere safe to keep all the precious little ornaments that Napoleon III's contemporaries loved to have cluttering up their homes. Incised glass was used for some especially high quality *vitrines*.

▶ *Tables, Bureaux, Consoles*

The family of tables is extremely large and varied. They come in all sizes and are modelled on every conceivable style. Large dining-tables are Neo-Renaissance whilst the many miniature tables tend to be imitation Louis XV or Louis XVI. We also find that the legs of tea, gaming or work tables vary between spindles, colonnettes and consoles, turned in the strangest manner imaginable. Table-tops are round, oval, kidney-shaped, square, rectangular or octagonal. They are decorated with marquetry, immensely varied inlaid patterns, glass plates laid over dried flowers, mosaics, *verre églomisé*, (see Glossary) leather or fabrics. Table-tops may be extended in many ways – into two or four sections, fan-shapes, etc. Occasional tables, nests of tables and light *guéridons* add still more to the number of tables designed for specific purposes. Many of them may be opened up to reveal writing-desks, drawers or secret compartments.

The craftsmanship of Neo-Louis XVI *bonheurs-du-jour* is particularly fine. The most precious woods of all are used to make them: purplewood, tulipwood, curly-grained walnut and ash root. They are delicately ornamented with painted mother-of-pearl roses, Sèvres porcelain plaques and other floral motifs (fuschia, convolvulus, etc.) painted straight on to the wood. There are also some *bonheurs-du-jour* in ebony with Boulle-style tortoise-shell and ivory marquetry designs.

Toilet tables appear in widely differing forms. The Pompadour style is the most luxurious type of toilet table. Its white marble top rests on abundantly carved and gilt turned legs; its frieze is fitted with drawers. More typical of the Napoleon III era, however, is the type of toilet table lacquered white and picked out in gold; it is plentifully adorned with clouds of frilly guipure lace. The average well-to-do bourgeois gentleman satisfies himself with a kind of large *commode à l'anglaise*, covered over by a flap to conceal the wash-bowl and toilet articles. In the bedroom, the mirror has now become an indispensable accessory to a lady's *toilette*. *Psychés* continue to be made, also smaller looking-glasses which have their place on the toilet table. However, the *armoire à glace* which came into existence under Louis-Philippe often dispenses with the need for either of these two mirrors.

Ebénistes also found themselves compelled by the new living conditions to create some extremely modest pieces, amongst which we might mention the umbrella-stand and the hat-stand. These much despised objects continue to be used during the Third Republic. Pianos and billiard-tables may also claim to have been the objects of some experiments in decoration. Billiard-tables are heavily overloaded with glittering bronze mounts. Pianos are decorated with marquetry designs or lacquer inlays.

▶ *Seat Furniture*

It is in this category of furniture that the *ébénistes* demonstrate their skill most effectively. Interiors are now invaded by masses of chairs of every description. Old forms are scarcely recognisable, since everywhere we find castors (see Plate xxxvii), button upholstery and additional braid trimmings. Woods of all kinds are used but they are still not sufficiently decorative in themselves; wrought iron, painted cast iron, wicker-work and *papier mâché* also enter into the manufacture of many seats.

The vogue for imitation antique seats resulted in some Henri II-style chairs being made in waxed walnut with straight backs, abundantly carved or leather upholstered. Castors terminating the legs are included. The most widely popular type of seat is that derived from the *chaises à la Reine* (see Chap. VI, p. 111). Uprights and traverses are turned and moulded; the front legs are slightly curved and terminate in shoes. The S-shaped back legs are continued upwards above the seat rail to form the back framework and the whole is surmounted by a 'basket handle' traverse; metal castors are fitted on to each leg. As far as arm-chairs are concerned, the arm-rests are set back on to the side rails; this position is just as suitable for Napoleon III crinolines as it had been for Louis XV panniered skirts.

The fashion for imitation Louis XVI furniture was at its height at the end of the reign. It was a modified version of the true Louis XVI, as we can see from Jeanselme's copy of an arm-chair originally executed by Foliot in 1774. In fact it amounted to a compromise between Louis XV and Louis XVI. The 'Voltaire' arm-chair appealed to Napoleon III's contemporaries for its comfort, hence it continued to be made under the Second Empire. The same applies to all gondola-shaped seats.

Smaller chairs appear in many different forms, often contriving to avoid imitation of any one precise style. For instance there are wicker-work or bamboo chairs, or even some in mock bamboo made in a manner to suit the material chosen. The custom of carving twisted cord and bows in wood also gives rise to some highly original stools and chairs. Again, neither the Louis XV nor the Louis XVI styles can truly be said to have inspired those chairs with extremely flimsy legs and pierced backs (slender colonnettes, traverses or medallions) made in a dark wood with inlaid fragments of mother-of-pearl, *papier mâché* or gilt wood.

▶ *New Types of Furniture*

The easy chairs of this era represent the triumph not of the *ébénistes*, but the *tapissiers*. We might say that the Second Empire is characterised by its fully upholstered, buttoned or 'fringed' seats.

The *crapaud*, a small, low, dumpy arm-chair, had already made its appearance in the previous period. It continues its brilliant career, upholstered in the most vivid rainbow colours. *Canapés*, fitted with braid fringes and submerged beneath piles of cushions, are installed in every well-to-do drawing-room. Pouffes, those low, round, backless seats with their fringes hanging right down to the ground, can be found in every room. When the pouffe swells to over-large proportions it is provided with a central cylindrical back; in this case it becomes a kind of divan called a *borne*. Some models can be split into two parts and placed back to the wall on occasions when they would be too cumbersome in the middle of the room. The *confidant* is a rectangular pouffe divided into two seats by a low S-shaped back (see Plate xxxvii). There are even some 'indiscreet' versions extant with curved zigzag back enabling three people to sit together.

▶ *Beds*

Beds are nearly all made in hybrid styles. They are usually modelled largely on the French Renaissance types but other styles are included. The bed belonging to Empress Eugénie at Saint-Cloud is an excellent example of such composite furniture. The Louis XV style provides a basis for some structural parts of beds (backs) and some decoration (carving and ornamentation on the tester and backs), but we see the Louis XVI style reflected in the slender fluted and cabled colonnettes, in the small square blocks at the ends of cornices and in the rows of fluting. The Napoleon III era added its own fringes, tassels and button-upholstered backs.

The vague overall impression that Second Empire artists failed in their mission has merely succeeded in furthering the bad reputation of Napoleon III furniture. In continuing to lead furniture astray into the wilderness of disastrous *pastiche* they delayed the emergence of a new style. This made it extremely difficult for their successors to produce new work after twenty years of industrial imitation had killed the general public's taste for novelty. The artists who tackled the problem of revitalising furniture design in about 1880 have generally speaking passed harsh judgement on Second Empire work. Here for example is Emile Gallé's verdict: 'The men of my generation found themselves in a very awkward situation when they started their careers. Plenty of decorative art was being produced, there was even some highly competent work being done in France, and the *Monde Illustré* and *Magasin Pittoresque* have left us with pictures showing that all these men could do was to repeat the themes of the past. Some admittedly were so smitten with the Renaissance that not only did they forget they were modern but they even forgot they were French. Italy held such a fascination for them! Others virtually lived in the *Musée de Cluny*. A Cluniac style of furniture had grown up . . . just as there had been long ago, though I think it should more properly be called a Cluniac style of architecture.'[1]

However, we should not condemn Napoleon III furniture altogether. Those luxurious *ensembles* created at Saint-Cloud by the Empress Eugénie cannot have been devoid of charm. It is the badly designed, badly constructed, carelessly decorated, enormously mass-produced pieces which still filled *petit bourgeois* homes thirty years after the end of the Second Empire that have brought discredit on this period's furniture and have made us forget its undoubted good points.

CHAPTER ELEVEN

THIRD AND FOURTH
REPUBLICS

From 1870 to 1939 French furniture assumes many different
guises; since it is still so near to us we are probably prevented
from making an unbiased assessment of the attempts at
renewal which have taken place during the first three quarters
of this century. One fact alone is certain: the public took no
interest in the brave struggles made by a small group of
pioneers to give France an 'everyday' furniture, freed from all
servile imitation of the past. When groups of artists showed
their new works at the 1900 Universal Exhibition, visitors
were disappointed and disconcerted by the novelties presented
to them; sarcastic remarks passed by the most respected
critics of the day added nothing constructive; they neither
encouraged the artists nor directed their efforts. The artistic
rebirth took place therefore without the moral support of a
cultured clientèle; it also took place without the manufacturers' financial support; men of commerce and industry
managed their affairs solely in their capacity as businessmen;
aesthetic considerations were unimportant to them. If pseudo-
Henri II and pseudo-Louis XV sold well, why should they
change their manufacturing processes, whatever they were?
This is the reason why, right until the First World War, furniture in general household use stayed more or less the same as it
was in about 1870. The mania for *pastiche* that had become a
deep-rooted social convention after seventy years of intensive
industrial production, the intellectual *élite*'s unconcern with

the art of furniture design, and the manufacturers' obtuse attitude are probably all equally responsible factors in holding back the creation of a new style. It is difficult to understand how, in about 1920, a complete revolution in general furniture styles was in fact achieved unless we study the work of those pioneer artists who worked in obscurity, striving to free furniture from the slavery of the mock antique.

The gradual evolution of a new style came about in several phases; each date in this 'Renaissance' marks another step forward on the path to artistic rebirth. First of all, everything that existed previously had to be eliminated; this is what the artists working between 1880 and 1900 set out to achieve by guiding decorative art towards new forms. At the 1900 Exhibition we see them win their first round: furniture can and should be designed to answer the needs of modern life, and should not simply be made to adopt outmoded forms and decoration. The second generation of artists, who took up the cause from 1900 to 1910, set up new aims: firstly, to interest the general public in their efforts to renew art, through the medium of exhibitions, magazines, etc.; secondly, to secure the manufacturers' effective co-operation. The lead taken by some Munich artists who presented their work at the Autumn Salon in 1910 clearly demonstrated the need for such a three-fold collaboration to ensure that serviceable and durable furniture should be produced. After 1910, and despite the interruption of the war, this understanding between artists, manufacturers and the public finally began to bear fruit. New mass-production furniture appeared on the market and found buyers. It had taken sixty years (1860–1920) for furniture design to emerge from the impasse in which it had been caught since Louis-Philippe's reign.

The 1925 Exhibition therefore marks the beginning of another phase. Original creative work, which had lapsed for almost a century past, is now revived; the chain of development leading from the most glorious years in the art of furniture design is resumed; this time everyone – artists, customers and manufacturers alike – is agreed that a new style should be established. However, the artists were divided amongst themselves as to the basic principles which should govern such new work – hence the numerous and bitter disputes that arose. As before, when machine-tools first appeared, stylistic experiments had to be adapted not only to suit the new requirements of the customers but also to fit in with technical developments. Some method had to be found whereby the increasingly smaller apartments could be furnished to accommodate countless magazines, gramophone records, radio and television as well as all the photographic and cinematographic equipment beginning to pour into the home. Nowadays, materials recently introduced on the market not only make it possible to fashion new forms entirely without precedent but also new colour harmonies. Synthetic products, with their much more brilliant and varied colours than any which could be obtained from wood, enable us to combine white, yellow, green, blue, red, grey, etc. with perfect ease. There is also one last factor which comes into consideration: owing to the speed of modern communications and the vast number of journals published, decorators have very quickly been able to get information on current production in other countries. Instead of the strictly national characteristics of olden times, we now have what is virtually an international style. This is so much the case these days that it is becoming difficult to detect whether a piece of furniture has been made in France or in any other country.

A piece of furniture may enjoy some degree of temporary popularity through its impact of surprise or novelty, but it will never stand high in the estimation of future generations – whatever materials are used and whatever techniques are adopted – unless its creator has succeeded in establishing a masterly balance or perfect relationship between its function, its structural form and its decoration. The intrinsic value of furniture depends ultimately on this fundamental and time-honoured principle.

TRANSLATOR'S GLOSSARY
AND NOTES

BAS D'ARMOIRE A low cupboard, almost always rectangular, surmounted by a marble slab. The front may have one or two doors. It was sometimes referred to as an *entre deux* since it was often set against the wall between two windows.

BONHEUR-DU-JOUR Although this was, generally speaking, a small writing-table with the addition of a low paper-rack and drawers, used by ladies for writing an endless succession of notes, it was really a smaller, lighter version of a man's bureau and not an exclusively feminine article. Sometimes the drawer in the table-top contained compartments for cosmetics and a mirror. Perhaps the most graceful item of all Louis XV and Louis XVI furniture, it may have taken its name from its sudden and immense popularity.

BUREAU À CYLINDRE This can be translated as a roll-top or cylinder-top desk, depending on the way the shutter is constructed. If it is the earlier type (i.e. Oeben's *bureau du Roi*), with the shutter made up of linked slats which automatically roll away inside the body of the desk, wrapping themselves round a concealed cylindrical bar, it is of the roll-top type. Where the shutter is a rigid quarter-circle sheet of wood that merely slides back into the top of the desk, it is of the cylinder-top type. There is one exquisite example inlaid with lozenges of mother-of-pearl at Versailles. Both types were generally counter-weighted in order to spare the owner any effort in opening it. The *bureau du Roi* shutter, could – originally — be operated simply by turning the key in the lock.

CARYATIDS Full-length carved figures of women used as supports for any form of entablature (table-legs especially), imitated from the columnar figures on ancient Greek temples, e.g. the Erechtheum at Athens.

CHIFFONIÈRE Cabinets containing shallow drawers one on top of the other were common under Louis XV and Louis XVI and were known under the generic name of *chiffonières* because they were intended to hold garments of chiffon and other flimsy materials. There were also some *tables en chiffonnière* which contained drawers but were supported on tall legs, sometimes linked by a shelf. Some table-tops had a high gallery, elegantly pierced, to prevent balls of wool, etc., from falling off and might well be classified as work-tables or *tricoteuses*.

190

CIRE PERDUE The most primitive and commonly used method of making a mould for bronze-work, having been described by the monk Theophilus and by Benvenuto Cellini. The mould comprises a hard core of pounded brick, a wax model of the proposed bronze on top of that, and the outer casing, applied in the form of liquid clay and allowed to dry. Metal rods have already been passed from the core, through the wax and projecting beyond; these hold the whole mould together. When it is heated, the wax melts and runs out, molten bronze is then poured into the cavity. When it is cool, the casing and core are carefully chipped away.

ÉBÉNISTE Roughly equivalent to an English cabinet-maker, a specialist in veneered furniture. The French word *ébéniste* derives from the ebony with which most seventeenth century furniture was veneered. The *ébénistes* were chiefly employed at Court or by wealthy Parisians.

FAUTEUIL À COIFFER The top rail on the back of this chair was bent into a steep curve in order that a lady could lean back and have her hair powdered more easily.

FIGURES ON LOUIS XV FURNITURE In addition to the Chinese figures, the monkey acrobats and nymphs, we sometimes find quaint, doll-like figures from the Italian *Commedia dell'Arte* in their traditional costumes – Harlequin, Columbine, Silvia, Pantaloon, etc.

GUÉRIDON As well as being fitted with a series of shelves, *guéridons* could be made quite simply with just a small flat top and used as candle-holders; the support may also take the form of a Negro slave. It derives its name from a Moorish galley-slave named Guéridon.

GUILDS It was very unusual for one craftsman to practise both as a *menuisier* and as an *ébéniste*, though Georges Jacob was an exception. Most of them specialised in one or the other technique. It was a lengthy and expensive business to be admitted as a *maître* of the Guild. An apprentice would enter the workshops of a *maître* at the age of twelve or fourteen; he would be an apprentice for six years, during which time his parents would have to pay the *maître* for his maintenance. After this he would become a *compagnon* for anything from three to six years, but he could work for more than one *maître* and receive payment. Only at the end of this training could he hope to be admitted as a *maître* himself. Vacancies in the Guild were limited and admission fees were high. However, the King was empowered to create *maîtres* as he chose. The would-be *maître* would have to submit a specimen piece of work (his masterpiece) for inspection by his colleagues as proof of his skill. Once admitted, he could set up his own workshop as long as he obeyed the Guild's regulations. Similar Guilds existed for bronze-workers, founders, etc.

HUCHIER Literally a 'chest-maker', the all-purpose carpenter of the Middle Ages. A *huche* or hutch was a rough type of household chest.

JAPANNING The process of coating metal or wood surfaces with various varnishes which are subsequently dried and hardened by heat. It was a European imitation of Oriental lacquer but different from it considerably in technique.

MAQUETTE A miniature wax model of a piece of furniture as it would appear when finished. The *ornemaniste* would present his client with a *maquette* for approval before starting to work on the wood.

MENUISIER Roughly equivalent to a joiner – a furniture carver who specialised in working in solid wood and had his greatest triumph perhaps in the Renaissance. He would have made a wider range of articles in the Provinces because there veneered furniture was not so much in demand as it was in the more sophisticated surroundings of the Court or Paris.

MEUBLES D'APPARAT These are part of the general scheme of interior decoration and usually the grander items, i.e. thrones or special pieces for state occasions.

MONTGOLFIÈRE The pierced splat of this kind of chair was carved into the shape of a balloon to commemorate the first balloon ascent made by the Montgolfier brothers in 1783.

PSYCHÉ A cheval dressing-glass. A full-length mirror swinging in a free-standing frame and attached to column supports by swivel screws. The base was always heavy and widely splayed. It could certainly not be moved around easily. Another popular type of mirror during this period was the pier glass, which was always fixed to the wall between two windows.

SIÈGES MEUBLANTS AND SIÈGES COURANTS Chairs were divided by strict protocol into two classes according to the position they occupied in the room: the *sièges meublants* which stood against the wall, and the *sièges courants* which were dispersed around the centre of the room and could be moved around at will.

TABLE À LA TRONCHIN There is an excellent example of these ingenious multi-purpose bed-tables in the Metropolitan Museum, New York, made for the Queen in 1778 at Versailles when her first child was born. It is a combined reading-writing-toilet-table with elaborate mechanical fittings and concealed springs; the reading-desk, for instance, may be reversed on a swivel and is fitted on the inner side with a mirror. Théodore Tronchin was a highly fashionable Swiss doctor who lived in Paris in mid-eighteenth century.

TAPISSIER A specialist, not only in tapestry-work but also in all manner of floor coverings, upholstery-work, window and wall-hangings, especially during the nineteenth century.

TERMS OR TERMINAL FIGURES Carved male or female busts, usually gods and goddesses of ancient Greece or Rome, surmounting tapered quadrangular pedestals or pilasters. They were used to decorate uprights, especially tables or Renaissance *buffets*.

VERRE ÉGLOMISÉ A method of decorating the underside of glass with gold painted patterns devised by an eighteenth-century picture-framer named Glomi.

VIDE-POCHE OR VUIDE-POCHE A small table to take the contents of a gentleman's pockets on his retiring to bed at night. Coat pockets of the period were large and a gentleman would very likely carry several snuff-boxes as well as other small objects. It was often provided with drawers or a fire-screen at the back.

XXXVIII *Guéridon Table, 1902*

| INDEX

193

XXXIX *Sideboard, 1955*

Printed in Great Britain by
Cox and Wyman Limited · London · Fakenham · Reading